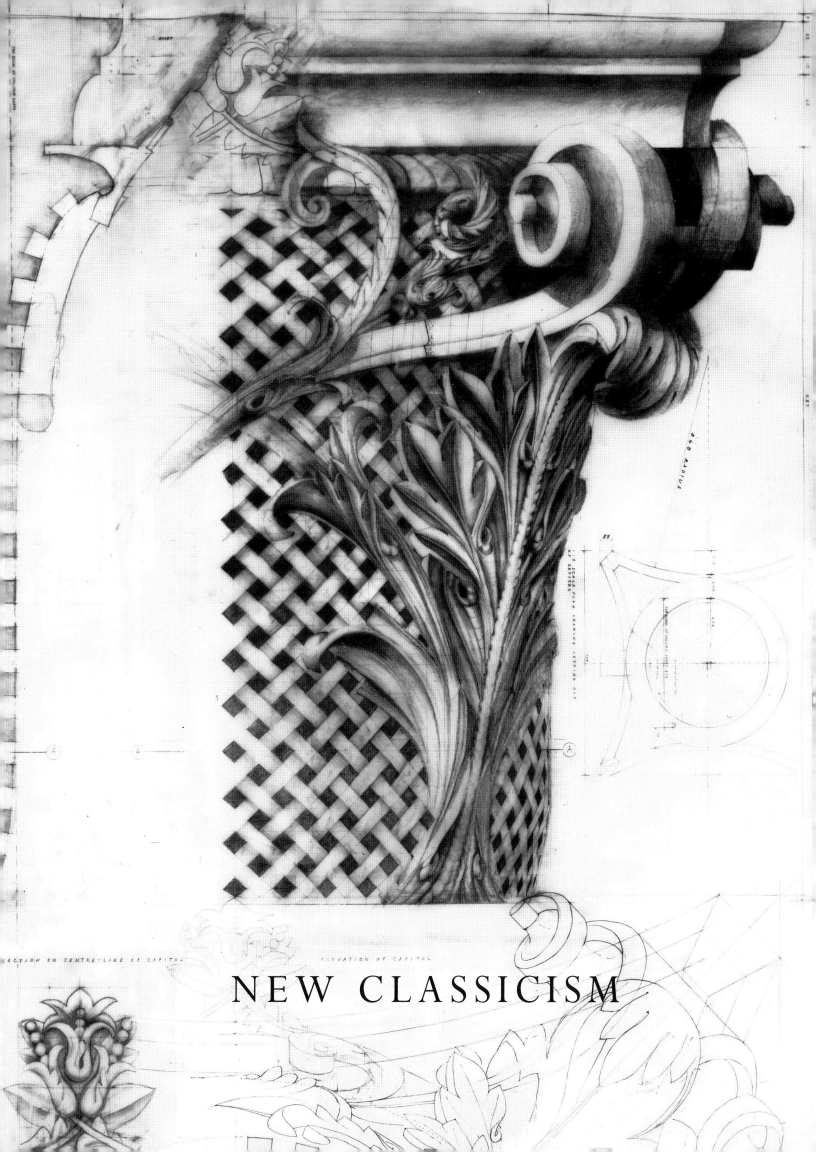

SECTION ON CENTRE-LINE OF CAPITAL   ELEVATION OF CAPITAL

NEW CLASSICISM

NEW

CLASSICISM

THE REBIRTH OF TRADITIONAL ARCHITECTURE

ELIZABETH MEREDITH DOWLING

RIZZOLI
NEW YORK

First published in the United States of America in 2004 by
RIZZOLI INTERNATIONAL PUBLICATIONS, INC.
300 Park Avenue South, New York, NY 10010
www.rizzoliusa.com

ISBN-10: 0-8478-2660-0
ISBN-13: 978-0-8478-2660-5
LCCN: 2004106432

Designed by Abigail Sturges

Printed and bound in China

2006 2007 2008 / 10 9 8 7 6 5 4 3

FRONT COVER: *Entrance Hall,
Residence, Harrison Design Associates
(see p. 172).*

BACK COVER: *Column detail,
Corinthian Villa, Regency Park Villas,
Quinlan & Francis Terry (see p. 88).*

HALF TITLE: *Freehand pencil drawing
by Francis Terry of new Corinthian
capital inspired by the Vitruvian
mythic source of an acanthus plant
growing into an offertory basket,
1989 (see page 88).*

TITLE PAGE: *Facade of Huckleberry
House, 1982-1985, Alan Greenberg
Architect (see page 144).*

DEDICATION: *Detail from Queens
Gallery, John Simpson & Partners
(see p. 110).*

To all my students

ACKNOWLEDGMENTS

I would like to thank the many individuals who helped make this book a reality, especially my contacts with the architects Diana Apalategui, Nina Bransfield. Tobie Corban, Trudy Coutts, Jen Lutz, Pamela Phillips, Natalie Staropoli, Nicky Walker, and Mac White. I would also like to thank the Georgia Tech Foundation for the grant that allowed me to interview in person the architects in Britain and many of the architects in America. I would also like to thank Michelle Moody, Elaine Luxemberger, Doug Allen, Geddes Dowling, and Meredith Dowling for their insightful comments on the manuscript.

CONTENTS

INTRODUCTION

ABOVE: *Beechwoods, 1992, Allan Greenberg (see chapter nine). The spiral stair adds monumental elegance to a compact house.*

OPPOSITE: *Farmlands, 2001, Fairfax and Sammons (see chapter six). The Temple-of-the-Winds-columned portico accents the timeless solidity of random range walls of local fieldstone.*

The Fall 2002 tenth anniversary of the Institute of Classical Architecture inspired the creation of this book. As part of the weekend celebration, a juried exhibition displayed magnificent hand-drawn renderings, widely varied scales of built projects from houses to community designs, sculpture, and furniture—all well-detailed examples of classical and traditional design. To clearly indicate the breadth of current classical architecture, their accompanying publication, *A Decade of Art & Architecture 1992–2002*, presented descriptions of firms in America, by region, as well as firms in the United Kingdom, France, and Italy. For the first time architects, sculptors, painters, and educators working in the realm of classical and traditional architecture clearly saw that this was indeed an international movement. This book is part of the continuing examination of current classical design, looking at representative projects of a limited number of architecture firms from America and Britain working in an idiom that appeared lost forever only two decades ago.

To understand the history of the current movement, the terms *classic* and *classical*, which have a variety of meanings and implications, demand a particular explanation in the context of this book. The concept of the classical is used in all fields of human endeavor to denote excellence, whether in music, literature, physics, mathematics, art, or architecture. For architects, the term *classical* alludes to the systematic language of columns, moldings, rhythm, scale, proportion, and human reference that Greek and Roman cultures developed for more than a thousand years. Just as Classical literature was based on principles of decorous expression, the architecture of antiquity also followed a broad set of rules that defined the detailing of public and private architecture. Recorded by the Roman architect and writer Vitruvius, these principles were revived as a dynamic new language in Renaissance Florence, and have remained in continuous use since the fifteenth century. Rather than placing any limitations on the expressive possibilities of design, the enormous flexibility of this classical language of detailing has resulted in six hundred years of creative expression. The reserved early Italian Renaissance, the inventive mannerist period, the grandeur of the baroque, the experimentation of the Regency, the exuberant American beaux arts—these widely varied styles share a common architectural language, a basic set of column types, moldings, proportions. Just as the details of the face—the eyes, ears, nose, and mouth—produce generally similar yet ultimately unique individuals, so too do the shared details of classical architecture result in unique buildings.

A relatively new addition to the English language, the term *classicism* dates only to the early nineteenth century. As its root, classic, indicates, this term relates to antiquity and the later stylistic periods based on the concepts of antique architecture. This book is devoted to current architects who are contributing to the ongoing expansion of the classical language of architecture. Designating their work "New Classicism" emphasizes their recent construction but, more significantly, their buildings indicate a renewal of classical principles in the design of residences, office buildings, symphony halls, libraries—all types of buildings that compose our cities. These architects believe that architecture that connects with community and mem-

ory is preferable to modernist architecture that aims to shock, disturb, and constantly reinvent itself. Their humanist principles inform a movement to design individual buildings and entire cities in a manner that reflects the concern for context and beauty that architects have shared for thousands of years.

CLASSICAL TRAINING AND ITS LOSS

With few exceptions, current traditional and classical architects are self-taught in the rules of historic design. This odd circumstance arose from a hiatus in traditional design instruction that occurred in American and most other Western schools of architecture around 1950. Prior to this time, the curriculum in architecture schools was largely based on the principles of the venerable Ecole des Beaux-Arts in Paris, the French school dating to the late seventeenth century. The formal academic training of architects in America dates to the opening of the architecture school at the Massachusetts Institute of Technology in 1868. The principles of the Ecole des Beaux-Arts shaped the curriculum at M.I.T because the program's founder, William R. Ware, had studied under Richard Morris Hunt, the first American trained at the Ecole, and one of America's most prominent architects at the time. Until the early twentieth century, the majority of architects were trained by working with established designers and builders as apprentices, a time-honored procedure in Western culture. Formal academic training inspired American architects to employ the sophisticated classical language of architecture, enabling them to design compositionally complex public architecture. As a result, America is enriched with such memorable public buildings as the Metropolitan Museum of Art, Grand Central Terminal, the New York Public Library, and Rockefeller Center in New York; the National Gallery and Pan-American Union in Washington, D.C.; and thousands of magnificent public and private buildings throughout America.

The first challenge to the beaux arts-inspired method of design came in the 1930s, when many professors from the Bauhaus, the modern craft-based school in Dessau, immigrated to America to escape persecution in Nazi Germany. Some found positions in architecture schools, where they taught the Bauhaus aesthetic of free-flowing space, large expanses of windows, flat roofs, no applied ornamentation, and use of nontraditional materials. Humanist concerns for beauty, scale, and symbolic expression were replaced with the new formulation that emphasized innovation and technological appearance. The teaching of architectural history was even forbidden out of an overwhelming desire to make a break with the past. By 1950, American academic programs had abandoned the teaching of the architectural orders and the beaux arts principles of composition. All that remained of the former system was a use of French terminology and the studio system of design instruction.

Introduction of the modern aesthetic coincided with the economic collapse of the Great Depression in the 1930s. Little was built during this period, and the prospect of economical design offered by the simplified forms of modern architecture appealed to cash-strapped public and private clients. The buildings thus created may not have been built to last, but they were serviceable and affordable. Following the end of World War II, when construction once again picked up, the new aesthetic of European modernism had continuing appeal as a fresh, clean image for a society remaking itself. Almost no public buildings and only a small percentage of residential work were designed in traditional or classical forms. Glass office buildings, libraries, and city halls replaced their elegant art deco and classical predecessors, while the ranch style house filled the growing suburbs. By the 1950s, the beaux-arts-trained architects still in practice were reaching retirement age, and the new generation of modern designers lacked their knowledge of classical design. The craftsmen who created the plaster moldings, stonework, wood carvings, and decorative ironwork were no longer needed for the creation of unornamented buildings. Without newly trained classical architects, and with the supporting system of trades also disappearing, the possibility of entirely losing the classical tradition became a reality. What the depression of the 1930s and modern design had not done to end a two-thousand-year-old tradition, age and lack of training was accomplishing.

HENRY HOPE REED AND CLASSICAL AMERICA

Although modern design had captured the academy, appreciation of modernism was never absolute in America. One of the earliest and most vocal critics of the aesthetic changes to the urban character of American cities was Henry Hope Reed. His book *The Golden City*, published in 1959, presented an assortment of modern and historic facades, entrances, lobbies, sculpture, and ornament in photographic comparisons that compelled the reader to question modern aesthetics. He wrote:

> The City of Contrasts offers a strange spectacle: What is called Modern shrinks before an exuberant tradition, for the most part classical. If we today are perplexed at the transformation brought about by the current fashion, future generations will be even more so. Already the unornamented buildings appear as products of a generation faded in its own time. Why do we have such a spectacle, we may well ask, why is such desolation reserved for our era? In a land of plenty, need for economy offers no explanation, nor have political forces tipped the scale. The age does smile on us, but we in our architecture, and in all the arts, for that matter, are unable to smile back. The answer seems to lie in the current fashion and the forces behind it.[1]

Reed founded the organization called Classical America in 1968 with the intention of promoting the languishing aesthetic he so admired. He conceived of this group as being dedicated to the continuation of the classical tradition in the arts of the nation. Classical America sponsored lectures, tours, and exhibitions through its headquarters in New York and its numerous chapters around the country. The organization influenced a wide audience through the "Classical America Series in Art and Architecture." The series comprised over a dozen out-of-print basic textbooks on classical design as well as new contributions to the research of classical architecture. The organization's annual Arthur Ross Awards publicly recognize the architects, painters, sculptors, artisans, educators and patrons whose achievements and contributions help preserve and advance the classical tradition. Since its inauguration in 1982, over 150 individuals and organizations have been recognized for their efforts within the classical arts.[2] The first architects and artists recognized were from the generation educated in the classical tradition and consequently of an advanced age. The comparative youth of current award recipients indicates the growing vitality of the classical tradition.[3] The organization continues today through a merger with the Institute of Classical Architecture that has strengthened both organizations.

MODERNISM QUESTIONED

Doubts about modern design as a satisfactory solution for individual buildings and urban planning resulted in numerous challenges to what had become the status quo in the field of architecture. In 1966, the Museum of Modern Art published Robert Venturi's influential *Complexity and Contradiction in Architecture*, which was drawn from his confrontation with historic architecture during his tenure as a fellow at the American Academy in Rome. Venturi's writing was the theoretical foundation for postmodernism. His "gentle manifesto," as he termed it, encouraged some readers to reevaluate modernism and prompted others to pursue their interest in historic architecture. Venturi wrote:

> Architects can no longer afford to be intimidated by the puritanically moral language of orthodox Modern architecture. I like elements which are hybrid rather than "pure," compromising rather than "clean," distorted rather than "straightforward," ambiguous rather than "articulated," perverse as well as impersonal, boring as well as "interesting," conventional rather than "designed," accommodating rather than excluding, redundant rather than simple, vestigial as well as innovating, inconsistent and equivocal rather than direct and clear. I am for messy vitality over obvious unity. I include the non sequitur and proclaim the duality.
>
> I am for richness of meaning rather than clarity of meaning; for the implicit function as well as the explicit function. I prefer "both-and" to "either-or," black and white, and sometimes gray, to black or white. A valid architecture evokes many levels of meaning and combinations of focus: its space and its elements become readable and workable in several ways at once.

ABOVE: *Office of the Deputy Secretary of State, United States Department of State, Washington, District of Columbia, 1987–1989, Allan Greenberg Architect (see chapter nine). Dennis Collier carved the Ionic order.*

But an architecture of complexity and contradiction has a special obligation toward the whole: its truth must be in its totality or its implications of totality. It must embody the diffi-cult unity of inclusion rather than the easy unity of exclusion. More is not less.[4]

A further invitation to reevaluate mainstream architectural philosophy occurred in 1975, when the Museum of Modern Art in New York held an exhibit of renderings from the Ecole des Beaux-Arts in Paris. That the defeated rival would be ensconced in the temple of modern art clearly indicated that all was not well. In 1977, Arthur Drexler, the director of the Museum of Modern Art, served as editor for *The Architecture of the Ecole Des Beaux-Arts*. More than an exhibition catalog, this volume included scholarly articles by Drexler, Richard Chafee, David Van Zanten, and Neil Levine that revealed the philosophy and history of the Ecole to a new generation. In the preface, Drexler encouraged a thoughtful response to the exhibit:

> Some Beaux-Arts problems, among them the question of how to use the past, may perhaps be seen now as possibilities that are liberating rather than constraining. A more detached view of architecture as it was understood in the nineteenth century might also provoke a more rig-orous critique of philosophical assumptions underlying the architecture of our own time. Now that modern experience so often contradicts modern faith, we would be well advised to reexamine our architectural pieties.[5]

The failure of modern design to create a language comparable in depth and elasticity to the ones it had replaced led to a variety of stylistic experiments that attempted to address the short-comings of the dominant style. Postmodernism, high-tech, neorationalism, deconstructivism, computer-generated free form—all styles that reflected the desire for a more intellectually

complex and emotionally stimulating architecture. However, no modern movement since the 1930s has created a symbolic language of ornamentation that conveys both general and specific messages as successfully as classical architecture. Elaboration of form and material are mute by comparison.

SURVIVAL AND REVIVAL OF CLASSICISM

In the 1950s and 1960s few classical designers continued to find work, and those who did usually had small, mostly residential practices. Philip Shutze and James Means in Atlanta, A. Hays Town in Louisiana, and Raymond Erith in Britain are characteristic of this aging group of classical survivors. An early example of a public commission that spans from the survival to the revival of classical design is found in the unlikely renovation of a modern office building. In 1961 the State Department in Washington, D.C., opened its new brutalist headquarters and, immediately, a movement was initiated by Clement E. Conger, curator of the Diplomatic Reception Rooms, to transform the simple modern spaces of the eighth floor into a display of

the artistic heritage of the United States. As Paul Goldberger commented, "The most charitable thing that could be said about the sprawling, limestone-clad headquarters of the United States Department of State in Washington, D.C., is that it is a credible period piece from the late 1950s. It is also utterly banal, institutional, and graceless, suggesting the dreariness of bureaucracy more then the dignity of diplomacy."[6]

Several architects contributed their talent to the creation of this new suite of public rooms intended as a backdrop for events conducted by the secretary of state, vice president, and other members of the cabinet. From 1965 to 1980, Georgia architect Edward Vason Jones transformed a stark modern interior into a sequence of delicately scaled civilized rooms for the diplomatic receptions of heads of state, foreign ministers, and distinguished foreign and American guests. After Jones's death, Allan Greenberg continued the transformation of modernist interiors, as he described, into "rooms to reflect the continuity of American diplomacy and embody the noblest ideals of American life and culture."[7] From 1983 to 1989 the offices of the secretary and deputy secretary of state and the Treaty Room suite introduced an eighteenth-century aura to the otherwise nondescript building. Greenberg drew inspiration from American design, but, as is possible with the elastic language of classical design, transformed

the precedents to convey clearer nationalistic symbolism. In the tradition of Benjamin Latrobe's Tobacco Leaf Capital for the Senate rotunda, Greenberg created a Corinthian derivation he terms the Great Seal Order, after the Secretary of State's role as custodian of the nation's seal.

In 1984, John Blatteau was selected as architect for the Benjamin Franklin Dining Room, which would be the largest ceremonial room outside of the Capitol and the White House. This magnificent space creates a setting for dinners and receptions that equals in refinement the spaces available to European diplomats in their home countries. The twenty freestanding and twelve engaged Corinthian columns; the fireplace and draped windows are all inserted within the floor plate of a 1960's office building. One cannot imagine some of the nation's most important diplomatic dinners and receptions occurring in this building had it not been transformed from its original brutalist design.

SEARCH FOR CLASSICAL TRAINING

By the 1980s two generations of young architects who had received modernist academic training lacked the foundation they needed to create historically inspired design. Commenting on this lack of attention to classical knowledge in current architecture curricula, Robert A. M. Stern wrote:

> Without a meaningful program of professional education within the architecture schools themselves, Classicism cannot resume its role as a transferable discipline for the practitioners of the future. Imagine a university that would call itself serious but not have a Classics Department. Yet, in almost all architecture schools today, the Classical tradition is virtually ignored, its history barely addressed in broad surveys; and its language, the grammar and syntax that have structured every Western stylistic movement since the Renaissance, including early or so-called canonic Modernism itself, is completely ignored.[8]

The architects whose work appears in this book demonstrate the variety of classical training gained outside of formal architectural education in England and America. In the last

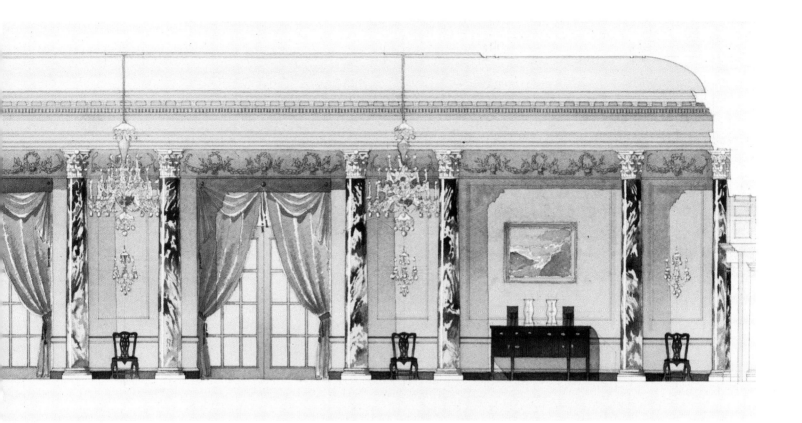

decades of the twentieth century, solitary professors passing on basic knowledge of traditional principles offered random university courses in classical and traditional design.[9] Finally, in 1989, the systematic teaching of classical design was reintroduced in the architecture program at the University of Notre Dame under the leadership of its new director, Thomas Gordon Smith. Earlier Smith had taught a single course in classical principles at the University of Illinois in Chicago, but Smith's position at Notre Dame, in concert with the design faculty, offered the opportunity to develop a form of training not seen for fifty years.[10]

The program at the University of Notre Dame is not a revival of old methods of design instruction; instead a modern curriculum that represents an inclusive rather than exclusive

ABOVE: *Watercolor rendering by John Blatteau of his winning competition entry for the Benjamin Franklin Dining Room, United States Department of State, Washington, District of Columbia, 1984. (see page 76)*

BELOW: *Rear elevation of Bond Hall, the School of Architecture, University of Notre Dame, renovation and addition by Thomas Gordon Smith, 1997.*

THIS PAGE AND OPPOSITE: *Master's Thesis project, "Conversion of Philip Shutze's Springhill into a Decorative Arts Museum," Jonathan Lacrosse, 2003, School of Architecture, University of Notre Dame. Pencil and watercolor.*

LEFT: *Title block inspired by Roman cinerary chest.*

BELOW: *Reconstruction of living room from drawings of proposed Thomas K. Glenn House, Sea Island, Georgia.*

OPPOSITE: Analytique *of period room installation for decorative arts museum project. Bulloch-Habersham House, demolished 1916.*

Architrave of Door

Cornice

THE BULLOCH-HABERSHAM HOUSE
1819 WILLIAM JAY · ARCHITECT

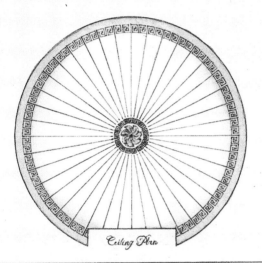

Ceiling Plan

Base-board

Elevation of Typical Window

Elevation of Fireplace Wall

Elevation of Door

The Bulloch-Habersham House in Savannah, GA was torn down in 1916. These Elevations and Details represent a conjectural reconstruction of the Breakfast Room. It is intended that this room be recreated for use in a Proposed Decorative Arts Museum for Atlanta, GA.

0 2 4 6 8 ins.

Scale for Details

SECTION AND DETAILS
of
THE CIRCULAR BREAKFAST ROOM

Drawn by Jonathan Wills La Crosse

0 2 4 6 8 10 fd

Scale for Elevations

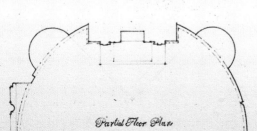

Partial Floor Plan

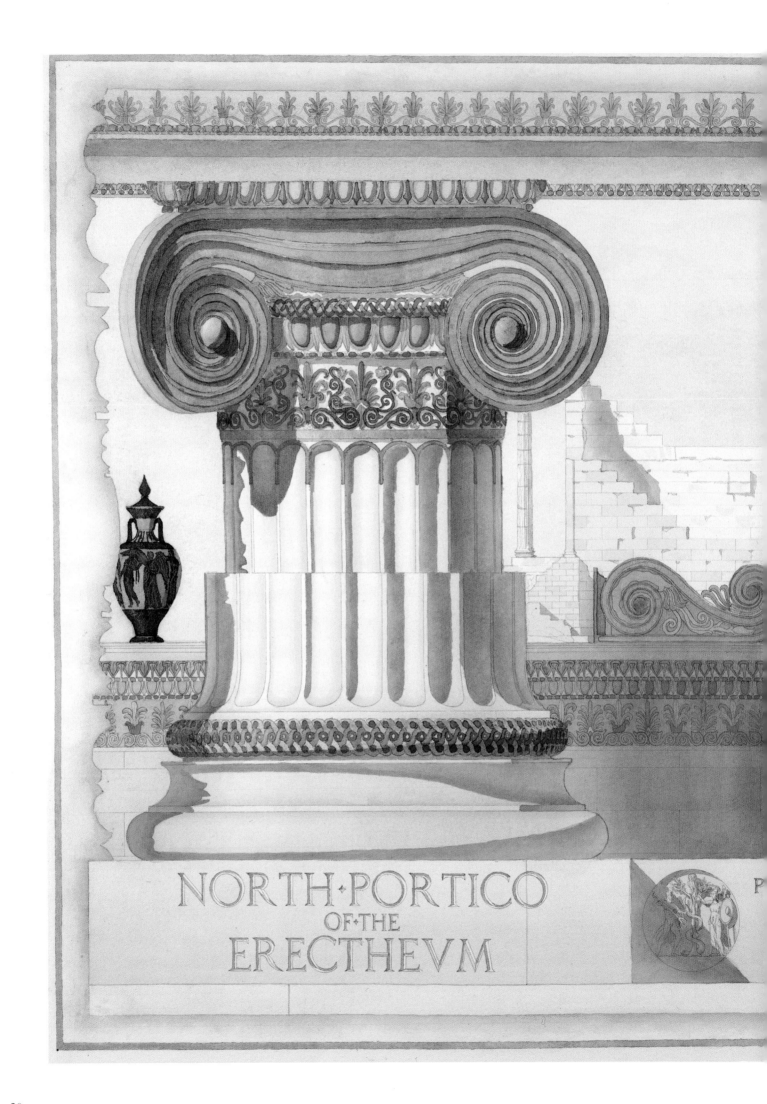

NORTH·PORTICO
OF·THE
ERECTHEVM

OF·P·PAJARES   DOM·FORTE   FALL·MMII

VNIVERSITY·OF·NOTRE·DAME
SCHOOL·OF·ARCHITECTVRE

viewpoint prepares students for contemporary practice. Consideration of context as an appropriate urban response is emphasized in studio problems. This understanding is further honed by the required year for undergraduate students and required semester for graduate students at their school in the historic heart of Rome. There the students are immersed in analyzing the character of a historic city and learn by example how design successfully enhances urban life. This sensitivity to contextual design is an obvious characteristic of the work of all of the program's graduates. The curriculum balances such topics as modern structural systems with knowledge of traditional forms of construction such as masonry bearing walls. Such inclusive knowledge allows the selection of sustainable and environmentally appropriate materials and systems based on a deeper understanding of their underlying principles, rather than merely relying on the current choices at hand. The students are also taught drawing, watercolor rendering, and computer-aided drafting, maintaining a balance of current and time-honored technique.

PRECEDING PAGES: Analytique *by Domiane Forte, first year graduate student in Paloma Pajares studio, 2002, School of Architecture, University of Notre Dame. Pencil, ink, and watercolor.*

The college-aged student could now receive proper classical training from Notre Dame, but those architects already in practice desired educational opportunities as well. This void in professional education led Richard Cameron and Donald Rattner to imagine an organization that would function like the T-Square Clubs of the 1920s.[11] In relating the origins of what would become the Institute of Classical Architecture, Richard Cameron wrote:

> In 1991 there was almost no place in New York for architects and designers to study the manual skills and intellectual foundations of classical architecture. We thought that there ought to be. It seemed such an obvious idea for those of us who had attempted to cobble together an education for ourselves with old books and the good luck of encountering great teachers here and there. We wanted to start a school of architecture based on the old Beaux-Arts ideal of practicing architects teaching working students and we had the audacity to believe we could make such a school out of nothing more than our will. I think we probably thought it might take a couple of years. Ten years later, the Institute is both less than we ambitiously imagined and much more than we had any reason to hope.[12]

The Institute, like traditional and classical architecture, is flourishing. Its activities include courses, a yearly journal, and thematically focused study tours. The Institute publishes a respected journal, *The Classicist*, which includes peer-reviewed scholarly papers, examples of student work, recently constructed buildings, and urban designs. Their first instructional program, a six-week intensive summer course in New York City, continues to provide educational enrichment for students and professionals. Extensive offerings of shorter evening and weekend courses cover both basic and advanced information on classical design.[13] In addition, travel/study trips in Europe and America, exhibitions, and a lecture series of internationally known architects and historians occur regularly in the New York headquarters and on the chapter level around the country. In 2002, the Institute of Classical Architecture and Classical America merged to acknowledge the similarity of their missions and to draw strength from the combined organization.

In the 1980s in Great Britain, a similar disenchantment with modernism became a formal movement. The Prince of Wales was the leading voice in the growing concern with the urban failures of modernism. In 1988 the BBC Television produced "A Vision of Britain," which focused on Prince Charles's opinions regarding the impact of modern architecture on the character of historic sites, especially Paternoster Square, with its 1950s development surrounding St. Paul's Cathedral in London. The following year this program's information was published as a book by the same name and authored by Prince Charles, whose continuing interest in improving the quality of his country's urban life led to the creation of The Prince's Foundation. Operating under the sponsorship of the foundation are several initiatives: The Urban Villages Forum, which actively works with communities in the redesign or extension of a village; the Visual Islamic and Traditional Arts Program, which sponsors postgraduate studies in the philosophy and practical skills of craftsmanship; The Prince's Drawing School, which teaches figurative art on a postgraduate level; the Regeneration Through Heritage program which is devoted to the reuse of abandoned or underutilized historical industrial buildings; and the Phoenix Trust which assists in finding new uses for the thousands of abandoned mills, factories, and dockyards in Britain.[14]

The Prince's efforts have resulted in numerous interventions in the historic fabric of Britain, perhaps most significantly in the redesign of Paternoster Square. Buildings of a scale and detailing that respectfully defer to their historic context have replaced the nondescript modern buildings that filled in the war-damaged area around St. Paul's Cathedral. Demonstrating even greater sensitivity to place, the historic medieval street pattern, as advocated by John Simpson, has also been reinstituted. The architects, craftspeople, and urban design teams working in concert with The Prince's Foundation are helping heal the British version of modern discontinuity.

REASSESSING THE DESIGN OF COMMUNITIES

In the United States, the destructive effects of modern interventions on the urban scale were first addressed in Jane Jacobs's *The Death and Life of Great American Cities* (1961). In 1977, Charles Jencks's *The Language of Post-Modern Architecture* dramatically dates the death of modern architecture to July 15, 1972, at 3:32 P.M., when the award-winning Pruitt-Igoe Housing (1952–55) in St. Louis, Missouri, was demolished. Jencks's book popularized both the term *post-modern* and the public dissatisfaction with modern design.[15]

In the United States a widespread effort termed "New Urbanism" continues to influence the design of new towns and neighborhoods, as well as zoning laws in existing cities. Andreas Duany and Elizabeth Plater-Zyberk initiated this movement to reconsider traditional urban design embodied in their groundbreaking design of Seaside, a "new community" in Florida. Based on building guidelines drawn from historic planning principles and local vernacular house forms and materials, the Seaside concept has influenced urban design throughout the United States. The general movement to which these design concepts belong has an organized philosophy defined by the "Charter of the New Urbanism." The charter states in part:

> We advocate the restructuring of public policy and development practices to support the following principles: neighborhoods should be diverse in use and population; communities should be designed for the pedestrian and transit as well as the car; cities and towns should be shaped by physically defined and universally accessible public spaces and community institutions; urban places should be framed by architecture and landscape design that celebrate local history, climate, ecology, and building practice.[16]

Although the theory of New Urbanism does not specifically advocate the use of historic architecture, many of the movement's concepts derive from the successful scale and detailing found in small towns and from the nostalgia for the individuality inherent in traditional neighborhoods and towns. Many award-winning New Urbanist communities respect their context of region and building style, rather than expressing the modernist emphasis on contrast with the surrounding context. The principles of New Urbanism encourage designers to consider both the individual building and the greater context in which it exists and produce buildings that mend the disjointed fabric of our cities.

NEW CLASSICISM

A new international award sponsored by Richard H. Driehaus gives recognition to major contributors in the field of classical and traditional architecture or historic preservation. The first of the annual Richard H. Driehaus Prize for Classical Architecture was awarded in 2003 to Leon Krier for, among many contributions, "his passionate advocacy of traditional architecture and urbanism." The 2004 Driehaus Prize was awarded to Demetri Porhyrios for his contributions to architecture as an architect, theorist, and educator. The $100,000 prize equals the formerly unmatched Pritzker Prize, given for modern architecture.

The architects and projects featured in this book embody a vigor in classical design. The work is representative of what may be found in current public and private work throughout the United States and Britain. Many modern architects assume only residences are currently designed in the classical language, but clients are equally interested in classically and tradi-

FOLLOWING PAGES: Analytique *of courtyard reconstruction of the Tempietto by Domiane Forte, 2002, School of Architecture, University of Notre Dame. Pencil, ink, and watercolor.*

tionally designed museums, libraries, office buildings, symphony halls, collegiate buildings, and residences. Another misconception surrounds the use of current structural systems and materials: all of the designers featured here accept certain aspects of modern design. The twenty-first century is a culturally and stylistically eclectic period. For the variety of scales and programs needed throughout the world, many forms of architecture are appropriate. However, within the design profession, uneasiness exists concerning historically based design. The presentation of a highly illustrated book is purposeful. Vitruvius directed architects to satisfy three demands for good building: firmness, or lasting construction; commodity, or appropriate function; and delight, or beauty. Many current buildings satisfy firmness and commodity, and the projects featured in these pages demonstrate that timeless beauty has returned to the architect's vocabulary. Perhaps the attribute of "new" classicism will be unnecessary because the continuity of classical history will be restored. The structure is being created for a new generation of trained architects, craft workers, muralists, sculptors, and professors who will hand on their knowledge to the next generation, as has been done by classicists for thousands of years.

1 Henry Hope Reed, The Golden City (New York: Doubleday & Company, 1959), p. 46.
2 http://www.classicist.org/rossawards.html.
3 Philip Shutze received the first Arthur Ross Award for architecture in 1982 at the age of ninety-two; Ferguson and Shamamian received the 2003 award.
4 Robert Venturi, Complexity and Contradiction in Architecture (New York: Museum of Modern Art, 1966), p. 22.
5 Arthur Drexler, ed., The Architecture of the Ecole des Beaux-Arts (New York: Museum of Modern Art, 1977), p. 8.
6 Paul Goldberger. "Allan Greenberg's rooms in the Department of State," Antiques. July 1987, p. 133.
7 Allan Greenberg: Selected Works (London: Academy Editions, 1995), p. 37.
8 Henrika Taylor, et al., eds. A Decade of Art & Architecture 1992–2002 (New York: ICA/CA, 2003), p.6
9 Architects teaching a variety of classical design courses include John Blatteau at the University of Pennsylvania and Drexel University, Elizabeth Dowling at the Georgia Institute of Technology, Francois Gabriel at Syracuse University, Allan Greenberg at Yale and Columbia Universities, and Robert A. M. Stern at Columbia and Yale Universities.
10 Jane A. Devine, ed. 100 Years of Architecture at Notre Dame (South Bend, Indiana: University of Notre Dame, 1999), p. 61.
11 T-Square clubs were popular in the first decades of the twentieth century. They were loosely organized evening schools for draftsmen without college educations. Skills in design were taught by practicing architects who enjoyed the social aspect of reliving their college days in the studio or their own time at the Ecole des Beaux-Arts.
12 Henrika Taylor, et al., eds., A Decade of Art & Architecture 1992–2002 (New York: ICA/CA, 2003), p. 9.
13 The course list includes both permanent courses and elective offerings. Among the courses offered in 2003 are the study of the orders, stone and wood carving, geometric proportioning, theories of classical architecture, elements of traditional urbanism in New York City, and drawing courses in watercolor, oil, and pencil.
14 http://www.princes-foundation.org/index.asp.
15 Charles Jencks, The Language of Post-Modern Architecture (New York: Rizzoli International Publications, 1991), p. 9.
16 The Charter of the New Urbanism may be found at http://www.cnu.org/about/index.cfm.

ROBERT ADAM
ARCHITECTS LTD.

ABOVE: *Detail of Library, British School at Rome, Italy, 2002, Robert Adam Architects Ltd.*

OPPOSITE: *New Lecture Theatre entrance, British School at Rome, Italy, 2002, Robert Adam Architects Ltd. Rusticated walls and bold voussoirs continue the spirit of the original building by Sir Edwin Lutyens.*

With offices in Winchester and London, Robert Adam Architects is the largest architectural practice specializing in classical and traditional design in Britain. Although the firm dates to 1955, the office's changing focus prompted the creation of the current firm name in 1993 with an organization of four directors— Robert Adam, Nigel Anderson, Paul Hanvey, and Hugh Petter. The firm's work includes new design, additions to historic buildings and master planning of new towns and speculative housing. Their projects may be found in the United Kingdom, the Bahamas, Italy, and Japan.

The principal architect, Robert Adam, received his architectural training at the University of Westminster in London. The focus of this school is both design and building technology, and Adam's training there encouraged him to take an open approach to the use of historic elements in new design. Like other architects of his generation, Adam received in-depth academic training in the rational scientific face of architecture, but relied on self-training in classical and traditional design. He received a Rome Scholarship in 1973 from the Architects Registration Council for the United Kingdom, which allowed him to develop his personal understanding of classical architecture.

Adam distinguishes his approach from those he refers to as literal classicists through his acceptance of modern technology. He disagrees with both the modernists' claim of technology as their sole domain as well as the literal classicists who shun techniques other than traditional forms of construction. Recent work includes a solar house that employs the latest technology, yet is humanized with forms that refer to the traditional images of home. With respect to his approach to design, Adam has written, "The classical tradition has been revived again, but in a quite different way and with quite different attitudes to those of the Classicism which was destroyed in the middle of this century. With the inheritance of Modernism always in the background, how can an understanding of invention and Modernity in the classical tradition help us to take classical architecture into the next millennium?"[1]

Adam is one of the most prominent figures in traditional design due to his own writing and his broadcast appearances. His book, *Classical Architecture: A Complete Handbook*, published in 1990, was one of the first late-twentieth-century works to augment the tradition of publishing measured architectural details that began in sixteenth-century Italy. This important book provides stylistic history, explanation of the orders, building elements, and functional types. In *Classical Architecture*, Adam explained, "Like literature, a classical design can take many forms and can be expressed in countless different ways. Like a great novel, a great classical building will have a simple message for everyone while offering the knowledgeable spectator layer upon layer of more profound meaning."[2]

ROBERT ADAM ARCHITECT

RESTORATION AND ADDITIONS TO THE BRITISH SCHOOL AT ROME

Rome, Italy, 2002

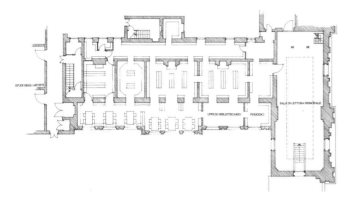

Hugh Petter, a director of Robert Adam Architects, created a master plan for the phased renovation and restoration of the original 1911 building designed by Sir Edwin Lutyens. The work includes a new addition on the front façade and the expansion of the Packard Library Wing, which houses over fifty thousand volumes, including an important collection of documents on the topography of Rome. Petter, a former Rome scholar, uncovered Lutyens's original plans for an unbuilt colonnaded veranda while preparing his 1992 book, *Lutyens in Italy*. Since he used this design to inspire his library expansion, the firm secured planning permission, often difficult to obtain, for new work in a sensitive part of Rome. The coupled Doric columns and pilasters follow Lutyens's detailing, but are rendered in a modern material made of cast marble dust colored with traditional color wash techniques. For the single-story extension on the historic front facade, Petter respectfully used a rusticated base and an exuberant door surround in the manner of Lutyens. The local Italian firm of Garofalo Miura Architetti added a new theater with modernist detailing.

YORK PLACE

Weybridge, Surrey, England, 1998

Located at the high point of the ancient village green, York Place complements and extends the historic town of Weybridge. Designed as a traditional terrace, the four connected houses redevelop a significant space formerly occupied by an unused tavern. Recessed masses, changing rooflines, and various window types create a delicate diversity appropriate to the town, yet the shared slate roofs, stucco walls and stone detailing unify the block as a picturesque backdrop for activities on the green. The composition won the National Home Builder Design Award in 1998.

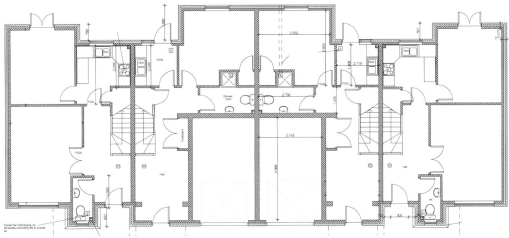

NORMAN DAVENPORT ASKINS

ABOVE AND OPPOSITE: *House in Central Georgia, 1998. Detail and view of rear stair hall with flying stair, constructed without apparent support from floor to floor.*

Norman Davenport Askins's firm in Atlanta is devoted to residential design and restoration and additions to historic buildings. His work may now be found throughout the United States. In 1966, Askins defied canonical modern design instruction by selecting the English Regency as the appropriate style for his bachelor of architecture thesis, thereby becoming one of the first of the new generation of American architects to publicly express interest in classical design. His professional training at the Georgia Institute of Technology was merely the beginning of a personal search for knowledge that would ultimately include a master's degree in architectural history from the University of Virginia, four years of detailed apprenticeship with the Colonial Williamsburg Foundation, and three years as director of restoration with John Millner and Associates, whose firm is one of the most respected architectural restoration firms in the United States. In 1977, Askins opened his own architectural practice in Atlanta, Georgia.

Askins is known for the exacting quality and authenticity of his details. While at Colonial Williamsburg, he worked with Paul Buchanan, the head of architectural research. In site visits to eighteenth-century houses, Buchanan taught his young apprentices how to dissect a building through careful observation of nail and brick fabrication, molding profiles, and rough and finish carpentry. From this accumulation of knowledge, the stylistic evolution of a house could be determined with no other documents than the building itself. Askins follows this training in the creation of new classical residences. Askins sometimes uses his clients' family history as a guide, or he may fabricate a new history for a project and then follow the logical sequence of a building's life as it responds to a century or more of change. For example, the family's size increases and a new wing is needed; the original mass of the house may have been built in the eighteenth century when Georgian was the high style; however, the addition is created after the Revolution, so the current design style is Federal. Such fictive histories allow Askins and the firm's other designers to make knowledgeable decisions on details to create a coherent design. Askins's work is also known for its fine craftsmanship. Like most traditional designers, he employs a set of craftsmen who understand his preferences and work easily with him as a team to produce exquisite details.

Askins believes that the greatest challenge faced by the contemporary classicist is the accommodation of new room types. He has pointed out that prior to the 1960s the organization of the family and its consequent use of rooms had not changed appreciably for centuries; therefore, a historic plan functioned well throughout most of the twentieth century. For today's traditional designer, the challenge is not technology, but new room usage, like family-breakfast-kitchen combinations, exercise rooms and spas, and extensive master bath areas.

HOUSE IN PALM BEACH

Palm Beach, Florida, 2000

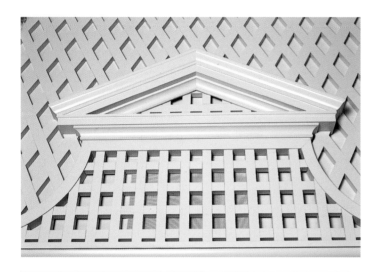

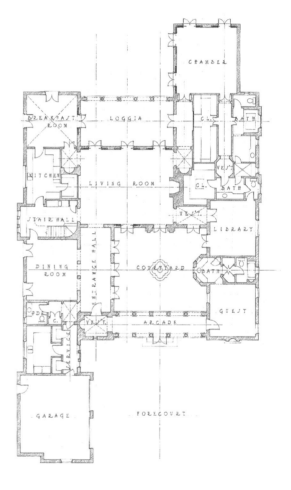

Over a period of twenty years, the clients of the Palm Beach house commissioned Askins to design projects for them in Georgia, Texas, North Carolina, and Florida. This house reflects their interest in gardening, classical architecture, and a desire for a generous but moderately sized house. To fit the site, the architects looked to the local vernacular of Addison Mizner, Marion Sims Wyeth, and Maurice Fatio, and created a home with massive stucco walls, coquina stone accents, and tricolor barrel tiled roof. To create a greater sense of space, axial views across gardens and water were emphasized. From the private parking court, an arcade leads to an enclosed courtyard with an antique Moroccan fountain and the ceremonial entrance door. Projecting quoins in a mannerist style add emphasis to the coquina entry surround. The interiors incorporate integrally colored plaster walls and ceilings and groin-vaulted vestibules, as well as pecky cypress paneling and beamed ceilings.

BELOW: *Rear loggia opening to lake view.*

RIGHT: *View of loggia from rear garden with hand-cut coquina columns and roof cornice.*

RIGHT: *Breakfast room trelliswork walls and ceiling inspired by porches and garden rooms designed by Elsie de Wolfe.*

BELOW: *Hand-wrought iron railing based on eighteenth-century Spanish precedent.*

OPPOSITE: *Dining room with pecky cypress ceiling in a star pattern inspired by early-twentieth-century Palm Beach houses. The floor is French limestone and the capitals and columns were locally carved in Florida.*

NORMAN DAVENPORT
ASKINS ARCHITECT

HOUSE IN
CENTRAL GEORGIA
1998

PRECEDING PAGES: *A preexisting pecan orchard provides the setting for the stucco-with-Texas-limestone-trim house. The trelliswork colonnade on the left connects with a pair of stone garage buildings.*

BELOW: *Ground floor plan.*

RIGHT: *View of south-facing garden facade with arcaded exterior living space.*

FOLLOWING PAGES

TOP: *Paneled walnut library in eighteenth-century-English style from material harvested, in part, on the family farm.*

BELOW: *View of rear curving hall with flying stair, looking toward entrance hall.*

OPPOSITE: *The living room is detailed with a mantel from Paris, silk covered walls, and leaded overdoors made with antiqued, mirrored glass.*

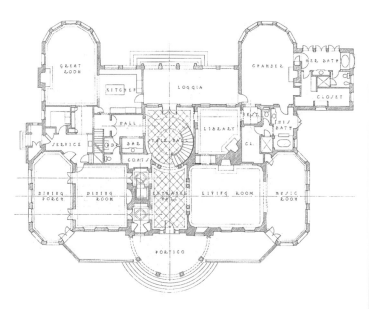

The lovely rural site with pond and mature pecan grove creates a quiet setting for this elegant house. The design is loosely based on Montgomery Place, a grand Federal-style house in New York. The clients requested a gracious formal house to accommodate large parties and periodic piano recitals given by the owner, a concert pianist. In response to this program, the house is composed of a series of geometrically shaped entertainment spaces. The principal cross axis terminates with the music room designed to accommodate two concert grand pianos. During recitals, the living room provides seating space. The entrance opens to a two-story hall with a flying stair designed by master stair builder Timothy Johnson of Franklin, North Carolina. The stair was developed from Johnson's collection of nineteenth-century German stair design handbooks. Like the German originals, the stair is made entirely of wood and, except for one wall connection, is freestanding from floor to floor.

JULIAN BICKNELL
& ASSOCIATES

ABOVE: *Detail of the library overmantel, Cranborne Manor, Dorset, 2000. Cranborne Manor has been a royal hunting lodge since the eleventh century. To celebrate the millennium, the seventeenth-century-wing library was refurbished with a new stone fireplace and overmantel featuring a limewood swag carved by Dick Reid, with animals and flowers drawn from Cranborne Chase.*

OPPOSITE: *Detail of the coved ceiling and giant Corinthian pilasters of the Hanover Room at Royal Crest House, Takasaki, Japan, 2002.*

Julian Bicknell is the principal of a London firm dedicated to the design of exquisitely detailed public and private buildings. His work includes projects in Britain, Japan, the United States, and Russia. Prior to opening his firm in 1983, Bicknell worked for Ted Cullinan, as director of the Project Office at the Royal College, and for Arup Associates. He received a master of arts and diploma in architecture from Cambridge University and later taught at the Royal College of Art. He was a founding trustee of the Prince of Wales's Institute of Architecture and served on the faculty from 1990 to 2000 as well as teaching at the Institute's summer schools in Italy, Germany, France, and the United Kingdom.

Bicknell began his career in the modern vernacular. His work on modifications of the historic Castle Howard in Yorkshire awoke a passion for classical design that was first expressed in his design for Castle Howard's new Garden Hall in 1978, which was created as a setting for the television adaptation of *Brideshead Revisited*. His first full-scale classical design was Henbury Rotonda, Cheshire, in 1983, which was inspired by a Felix Kelly painting commissioned by the owner, Sebastian de Ferranti. The design belongs to the English neo-Palladian style in the Vanbrugh manner. His first full-scale classical design was Henbury Rotunda, Cheshire, 1983, inspired by a Felix Kelly painting commissioned by the owner Sebastian de Ferranti. Explaining subtle aspects of the realized house Bicknell said, "The design belongs to a British lineage of English Neo-Palladian in the Vanbrugh manner. I have little sympathy or enthusiasm for Burlington. I believe he successfully extinguished the tradition of creative architectural thinking fostered by Wren in the generation of Hawksmoor, Vanbrugh, Gibbs, and Archer—a creative tradition that didn't revive until Dance and Soane a hundred years later."

Describing his own work, Bicknell has written, "Whether built or not, each design is the culmination of a long and sometimes tortuous process of evolution, the result of repeated trial and error, of careful consultation, second thoughts, and reversions to earlier ideas. Each is a creative exercise; each a learning process; each contributes to the store of knowledge and experience—on which subsequent designs may draw."[1]

Bicknell draws inspiration from early-eighteenth-century baroque and Palladian architecture, and has worked closely with the carver Dick Reid on decorative design features in a vivid early-eighteenth-century manner. The construction methods, however, are eclectic and contemporary, using concrete, steel, artificial insulation materials, and other contemporary technologies.

In addition to classical works, the office has undertaken several extraordinary projects that demonstrate an understanding of other styles and methods of construction. The Shakespeare Country Park of 1997 at Maruyama, Japan, includes half-timbered buildings and a functioning windmill; the unbuilt Knight's Castle in Gifu Prefecture, Japan, is a 2:3 scale reproduction of a medieval castle in stone; and a thatch-roofed vernacular cottage was built in Dorset, England. All of these display the same exacting care and attention to detail as the fine country houses for which Bicknell is best known.

JULIAN BICKNELL & ASSOCIATES

ROYAL CREST HOUSE
Takasaki, Japan, 2002

PRECEDING PAGES: *Entry court of Royal Crest House, Takasaki, Japan, 2002. New banqueting facilities adjoin a preexisting wedding chapel. This courtyard provides an elegant setting for secular festivities after the ceremony and for the final departure of the bride and groom after the banquet.*

RIGHT: *Banqueting room. Designed for ceremony and drama, the double stair cascade accommodates theatrical*

arrivals by the newlyweds from the second-story changing suite.

BELOW: *The entry hall connects the wedding chapel and banqueting hall. Stairs lead to the bar on the second story.*

FOLLOWING SPREAD: *Temple of the Winds columns accent the entrance linking the formal garden with the banqueting hall.*

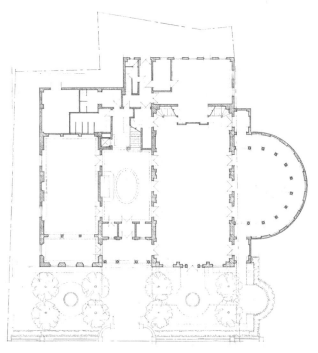

The Royal Crest House adds a banqueting complex to an existing wedding chapel and reception rooms. The building's earthquake resistant concrete construction is finished with painted stucco in a manner derived from early-nineteenth-century London buildings. The eclectic interiors reflect their various functions—a restrained Greek style for the reception room, a dramatic baroque for the dining room, and a wood-paneled bar.

JULIAN BICKNELL & ASSOCIATES

THE GEORGIAN CLUB

Tokyo, Japan, 1995

THE GEORGIAN CLUB

Tokyo, Japan, 1995

PRECEDING PAGES: *Main entrance, The Georgian Club, Tokyo, 1995.*

RIGHT: *Formal dining room.*

BELOW: *(bottom) plan of entrance and upper level of dining room; (top) second floor with club members private sitting room, library, and overnight suite*

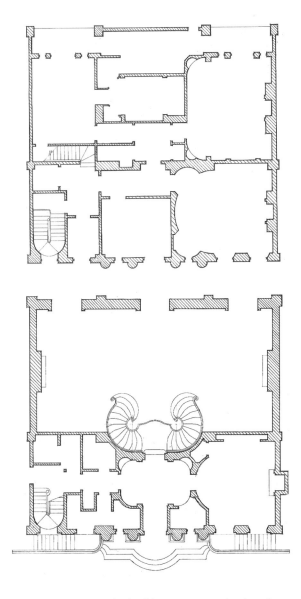

Located in central Tokyo, the building was conceived as the house of a mythical late-eighteenth-century aristocratic family and includes both a private residence for the owner and a private dining club. Members and their guests experience the amenities of a traditional London Club, with a classically detailed dining room, bar, sitting room, library, and a guest suite. The owner's apartment includes a roof terrace and private swimming pool. The Georgian design is rendered in concrete construction to satisfy Japanese earthquake codes. Dick Reid made the artificial stone Ionic capitals and entablature in the United Kingdom from original carvings. Richard Grasby made the frieze, which reads "Fortuna Domus Mea." Hayles and Howe of Bristol, England, created the elaborate interior plaster details, and County Forge, in Somerset, England, created the grand staircase and ironwork. Mary Fox Linton decorated and furnished the interiors.

JULIAN BICKNELL & ASSOCIATES

HIGH CORNER

Ashtead, Surrey, England, 1989

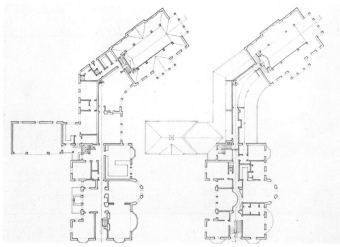

The five-bedroom house's irregular massing provides garden views for all major rooms. The formal rooms are axially aligned with the entry court and garden. The private wing, containing kitchen, family room, music room, and bedrooms, terminates with an enclosed swimming pool nestled within a private garden on the east side of the house. The house is detailed in Flemish bond brickwork with contrasting red rubbed brick arches and quoins. Dick Reid carved the hooded entry door with details referring to the house's owners.

JULIAN BICKNELL & ASSOCIATES

HENBURY ROTONDA

Cheshire, England, 1983

Situated as the centerpiece of landscaped park dating from the eighteenth and nineteenth centuries, Henbury Rotonda is designed in the neo-Palladian spirit appropriate to its setting. The concept of the house derived from a Felix Kelly painting commissioned by Henbury's owner, Sebastian de Ferranti. The interior rooms are symmetrically organized around the central hall, which rises fifty feet to the base of the lantern. Dick Reid created the reconstituted stone carvings cast from original molds, as well as the carved wood door cases and decorative features in the lantern. The pediment sculptures were made by Simon Verity and the stone letter cutting by Richard Grasby.

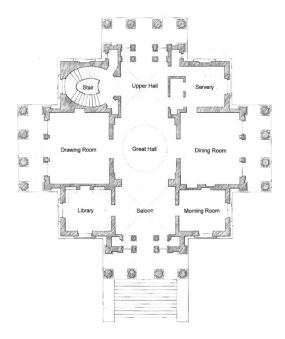

LEFT: *The oval spiral stair employs the traditional principle of interlocking treads that transfer the loads to the floor, not the wall, for support.*

OPPOSITE: *South end of the Great Hall.*

JOHN BLATTEAU
ASSOCIATES

ABOVE: *Ceiling detail, The Benjamin Franklin Dining Room, U.S. Department of State, Washington, D.C., 1984.*

OPPOSITE: *New entry pavilion, Paul Cushman III International Financial Center for the Riggs Bank, Washington, D.C., 2000.*

John Blatteau is a purist whose work reflects the expressive potential of classical architecture. Blatteau's knowledge of classical elements has been honed through twenty-five years of teaching at the University of Pennsylvania and Drexel University, a combination of theory and practice that, according to Vitruvius, is essential to the career of an architect.

Blatteau received three degrees from the University of Pennsylvania, an institution shaped in the first half of the twentieth century by the great French critic Paul Cret and in later decades by Cret's student Louis Kahn. While mainstream architects studied the current work of Kahn, Blatteau began assembling his future office library. His first purchases in 1970 of Letarouilly's *Les Edifices de Rome Moderne* (1874), and *Le Vatican et la Basilique de Sanit-Pierre de Rome* (1882), plus Durand's *Recueil et Parallele des Edifices de tout Genre Ancien et moderns*, (1833), came from the library of George Howe, a prominent Philadelphia architect and contemporary of Paul Cret. The use of documents to study a design problem connects Blatteau's work with the most respected traditions of classical design which emphasizes connections with great work of the past.

Through his self-directed study of the beaux-arts drawings at the University of Pennsylvania archives, Blatteau learned nineteenth-centry rendering techniques. The first recognition for his innovative approach came from the unlikely venue of the 1980 Progressive Architecture Awards. His detailed beaux-arts renderings of his design for the Bayonne Hospital, done with Stephen Bonitatibus, were probably the first such presentation drawings in fifty years and earned the project an honor award.

Blatteau opened his own firm in 1983 in Philadelphia. The young firm's first major project was won through a limited competition for the Benjamin Franklin Dining Room in the U.S. Department of State, Washington, D.C. This 1984 project marked the final phase of renovations creating the Diplomatic Reception Rooms begun almost twenty years earlier.

For his most loyal client, the Riggs Bank of Washington, D.C., Blatteau has produced over fifteen branch offices and more than 250,000 square feet of renovations, restorations, and new construction. Characteristic of his design approach, Blatteau has strengthened the classical ambience of the capital through his designs of respectful public buildings that visually weave the principal architecture of the eighteenth and nineteenth centuries with the modern city. Concerning his attention to detail, Blatteau says, "We are never particularly concerned with creating original works of art, but rather buildings that sit comfortably within their surroundings, appearing as if they have always been there."

Under the leadership of Paul Cret, the University of Pennsylvania had been the leading beaux arts-inspired program in the United States. This great heritage had been neglected until Blatteau rediscovered and passed along traditional information that few professors still understood. His teaching formed an educational link for his students to the vast knowledge of design, detailing the orders, and rendering.

JOHN BLATTEAU ASSOCIATES

PAUL CUSHMAN III INTERNATIONAL FINANCIAL CENTER FOR THE RIGGS BANK

Washington, D.C., 2000

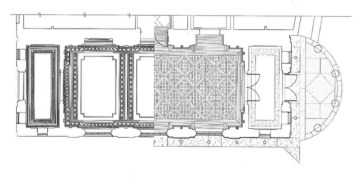

The Paul Cushman International Financial Center combines restoration, renovation, and new construction. The building includes the restoration and renovation of five 1920s-era, two-story commercial structures designed by the noted Washington, D.C., architect George Ray. The project also includes the addition of a new entry pavilion that completes the northern edge of the site.

The exterior of the entry pavilion employs limestone and granite detailed in a Georgian style. The scale and rhythm of openings complements the neighboring buildings, but its more elegant and pristine detailing clearly denotes it as the most significant structure in the block. The interior lobby is carefully detailed in a simple, refined composition of coupled Doric pilasters.

OPPOSITE (TOP): *The block prior to restorations and additions.*

OPPOSITE (BOTTOM): *New entry pavilion plan.*

THIS PAGE: *Completed renovation, restoration, and new construction of the block-long site.*

FOLLOWING PAGES: *New entry pavilion lobby.*

THE BENJAMIN FRANKLIN DINING ROOM

U.S. Department of State
Washington, D.C., 1984

PRECEDING PAGES: *Moving existing ductwork to the coved edge created space for the twenty-foot ceiling of the Franklin Dining Room.*

RIGHT: *Plan of the 45-by-90-foot Savonnerie-style carpet.*

BELOW: *Detail of the mahogany entry doors with flame veneer panels and hardware by P.E. Guerin. The scagliola columns imitate the small red Langueduc column shafts of the fireplace.*

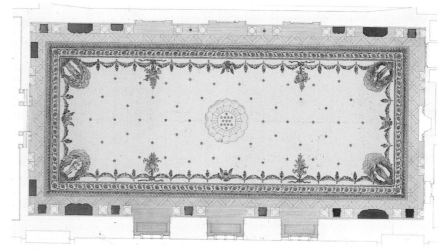

OPPOSITE: *White Carrara marble mantel and fireplace surround with column shafts and details of red French Languedoc. The bust on the mantel is an "original" terra cotta of the famous Houdon marble bust of Franklin.*

The final and largest addition to the Diplomatic Reception Rooms, the Benjamin Franklin Dining Room serves as the setting for state dinners and diplomatic receptions presided over by the president, vice president, and the secretary of state. John Blatteau developed two schemes for the invited competition—an Ionic Scheme, described by the architect as having a delicate and feminine sensibility in keeping with the Ionic order, and the selected Corinthian scheme, influenced by the designs of Robert Adam's Kedleston Hall, Percier and Fontaine's Ball Room at the Chateau de Compiegne, and their Grand Salle in the Tuileries Palace.

The twelve freestanding Corinthian columns—with partially gilded capitals, entablature, and coffered cove ceiling, eight Adamesque crystal chandeliers, and fourteen crystal wall sconces—create, as Blatteau has described, a room that is "an architectural celebration of grandeur and formal beauty." The decorative details in the central medallion and its reflection in the Savonnerie-style rug relate to the secretary of state's role as custodian of the country's Great Seal. The Diplomatic Reception Rooms are located on the eighth floor of the brutalist-style State Department Office Building, finished in 1961.

QUINLAN & FRANCIS TERRY

ABOVE AND OPPOSITE:
Corinthian Villa, Regent's Park, London, 2003.

The firm of Quinlan & Francis Terry extends the lineage of classical design from the firm of Erith & Terry, which operated from 1968 to 2003. Quinlan Terry was born and brought up in the heart of the modernist movement: his parents were friends with Walter Gropius, abstract sculptor Barbara Hepworth, and brutalist architect Erno Goldfinger. During his high school years, his greatest interest was sculpture. During his years at the Architecture Association, from 1955 to 1961, he became increasingly disillusioned with modernism and longed for more traditional, classical, and stable values. Upon graduation, Quinlan's dissatisfaction with current design inspired him to work with Raymond Erith (1904–73), the most respected traditional designer in Britain at that time.

Francis Terry spent much of his childhood accompanying his father, Quinlan, on sketching trips, and his vacations from college were often spent working in his father's office. He received his architectural training at Cambridge University. After graduation he worked as an apprentice with Allan Greenberg and for a period explored a career as an artist. After a short time he realized the benefit of combining his interests in art and architecture. With his talent in figural art, Francis designs sculptural decoration, an essential element for continued vitality in the classical tradition.

Father and son share a philosophy emphasizing traditional materials, construction methods, and symbolic ornament as valuable solutions for modern architecture, but they have found, although infrequently, that a given budget may demand some nontraditional detailing. Their preferred material choices are not made merely to evoke a historic appearance, but also to express the ethical integrity that characterizes their work. For every project, the firm demonstrates the financial viability of traditional construction and traditional forms of light and ventilation when considered through the life of the building. Such concepts are in line with the most current environmentally conscious, or so-called green architects. In addition, his work has demonstrated that solutions for modern problems can be accomplished without resorting to the startling appearance of nontraditional design. In a 1987 speech for the Oxford Union Debate, Quinlan said, "We cannot think seriously of architecture without raising at the same time the fundamental question of man's life on earth . . . . let us build smaller and gentler buildings; let us make walls of solid brick or stone; let us roof them with slates and pierce them with sash windows of the kind that have recommended themselves to generations of Englishmen; let us use the Doric, Ionic, and Corinthian orders; and let us take inspiration from the wisdom of our forefathers, so that our buildings will be signs and heralds of a more natural, more stable and more beautiful world."[1]

The firm's commercial work includes mid-rise office buildings like Baker Street, London, 2003; multiuse complexes like Dufours Place, Westminster, 1983–84; and Richmond Riverside, outside London, 1984–87. His main public buildings are the new Brentwood Cathedral, and the new lecture auditorium and library at Downing College, Cambridge. The firm also designed the restoration of the three state rooms at No. 10 Downing Street as well as numerous country houses in England, Germany, and the United States.

Quinlan and Francis Terry have created buildings whose excellence assures their place among the masters of British architecture. The firm has received many awards including the Royal Fine Arts commission's Building of the Year Award for Downing College Library in 1994, the Philippe Rotthier European Award for the reconstruction of the City of Archives d'Architecture Moderne in 1984, and the Georgian Group's 2003 Best New House in the Classical Tradition Award for Ferne Park. Quinlan Terry received the 2002 Arthur Ross Award for Architecture from Classical America.

REGENCY PARK VILLAS

London, 1988–2003

BELOW (TOP): *Entry facade of Ionic Villa, 1990. A drawing in Andrea Palladio's* I Quattro Libri *for Signor Girolamo Ragona at Le Ghissole inspired the design of the villa.*

BELOW (BOTTOM): *Site plan of the Regent's Park Villas.*

OPPOSITE: *View of Ionic Villa from the Grand Union Canal.*

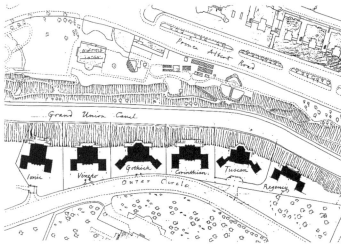

In 1988, Quinlan Terry developed a master plan for six villas located on the northwest corner of Regent's Park for the Crown Estate Commissioners. The individual designs reflect the picturesque tradition established in the nineteenth century by John Nash. Commenting on his method for developing the character of the six villas, Quinlan Terry says, "We step into Nash's shoes and keep walking." The Ionic Villa (1990), with its giant Ionic orders, combines Palladian and early Georgian concepts.

ABOVE: *The loggia (top) and drawing room (bottom) incorporate a Venetian influence upon traditionally English details.*

OPPOSITE: *The Veneto Villa (1991) is more refined, with stacked Doric and Ionic orders inspired by the Cornara Loggia in Padua by Falconetto, and a plan inspired by Palladio's Villas Badoer and Zena.*

The Gothick Villa (1991) was conceived as a
respectful nod to the stylistic diversity of John
Nash. The details are not of the nineteenth-
century Gothic Revival work of A.W.N.
Pugin or John Ruskin, but, as the name
implies, of the eighteenth-century "Gothick."
The crenellated roof, tall chimney pots, and
interior fan vaulting are drawn from the study
of such buildings as Horace Walpole's
Strawberry Hill and James Gibb's Gothic
Villa at Stowe.

Corinthian Villa (left), the final and most ornate, is influenced by the baroque style of Borromini and late Roman work. The alternating concave/convex curves of the facade draw upon the curves in Borromini's San Carlo alle Quattro Fontane, in Rome. For the first time in the history of English architecture, the triple curved, serpentine facade appears here on Corinthian Villa. For the columns, Francis Terry created an innovative new Corinthian capital by interpreting the Vitruvian story of an acanthus plant growing through the woven fabric of a basket. The spiral flutes add to the theatrical quality of the facade. All six villas are made of load bearing brickwork, natural and reconstituted stone details, and stucco walls.

The Tuscan Villa (not shown) (2001–2004) is the simplest in detail and finds its sources in the work of Inigo Jones. The Regency Villa (2002) and Corinthian Villa (2003) complete the site plan.

ABOVE: *Entry facade of Corinthian Villa, 2003.*

LEFT: *The spirit of Borromini is evoked in the curving entablature and perspective detailing of the front door and curved window above.*

ABOVE: *Entry facade of the Regency Villa, 2002.*

BELOW: *Doric detailing from the Parthenon is reproduced with great exactitude.*

QUINLAN & FRANCIS TERRY

20–31 BAKER STREET

London, 2002

PRECEDING PAGES: *The appearance of numerous individual buildings creates an appropriate scale for a 100,000-square-foot-office building in this historic area of London.*

LEFT (TOP): *The Ionic capital of the entry pavilion, carved from Portland stone.*

LEFT (BOTTOM): *Tuck-pointed brick (mortar matching the brick with a bead of white mortar) used on the corner building plays with the perception of size. Hand carved stone plaques, stone trim, and balustrade heighten the individuality of the large office floor plates.*

OPPOSITE: *The main entrance to the office building is marked by stone giant-order Ionic columns on a rusticated base.*

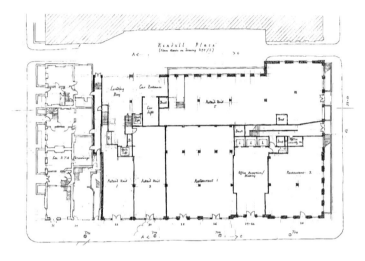

For two decades the client tried to develop the site with a modern scheme, but was unable to obtain planning approval. The traditional design and scale offered by Quinlan & Francis Terry's design received approval by the Westminster City Council and English Heritage because it answered the Portman Estate Conservation Area's requirements for the usage of classical details and construction. The external walls are made of solid brickwork with sash windows set in deep reveals. To satisfy the need for approximately 100,000 square feet of underground parking and connected office space, and to speed construction, the interior and roof were erected first in steel, allowing the load-bearing external walls to be erected at a slower pace.

The block-long office building achieves a compatible scale with the conservation area through its appearance as a joined series of smaller buildings. The principal entrance is denoted by the grander scale of the four giant Ionic orders above the rusticated and vermiculated ground floor rendered in white Portland stone. The corner building is made of tuck-pointed Rudgewick brick capped by a stone balustrade, a cantilevered first-floor balcony, and hand-carved stone plaques.

FAIRFAX & SAMMONS

ABOVE: *Rendering of Il Palmetto, Palm Beach, Florida, 2003, additions and renovations to an existing historic house by Maurice Fatio.*

OPPOSITE: *Entry loggia of Gulf Stream Residence, Florida, 1996*

The emergence of classical and traditional design as a major movement in twenty-first-century America is due in large measure to the dedicated partnership of Fairfax & Sammons. Richard Sammons was a founding member of the Institute of Classical Architecture (ICA) and an instructor at the Prince of Wales Institute in Britain in 1990. The firm's office also served as the headquarters for Henry Hope Reid's Classical America, the sole organization challenging modernist aesthetics until the establishment of the ICA in 1992.

The two architects received their academic training at the University of Virginia and pursued knowledge of classical design on the job: Sammons worked in Manhattan for David Anthony Easton, a classicist specializing in residential design, and Anne Fairfax returned to her native Honolulu to open a private practice. In Easton's office, Sammons learned detailing from Joe Marino, an architect who passed on the practical knowledge he learned in the firm of Cross and Cross, a prominent New York architecture firm. In Honolulu Fairfax designed classical vernacular residences inspired by the local work in Hawaii of Bertram Grosvenor Goodhue, David Adler, and Charles W. Dickey.

In 1992, they established their partnership to design exquisitely detailed residences. Of their work, Fairfax and Sammons have said, "We intentionally have no signature style ... we tailor everything to the setting, the climate, the owner's temperament. The work is about restraint, scale and proportion, not being self-conscious or calling attention to ourselves. We refine and refine the details to the utmost level possible, and always with an armature of proportional logic. In our work there are no arbitrary moves."[1] Their fifteen-person office, located in Manhattan's meat-packing district, includes the disciplines of architecture, interior decoration, and urban design.

Fairfax and Sammons employ the classicist's methodology of design: research of the most fitting precedents precedes abstract conception of design. For example, an image for a classical seaside residence developed from a variety of sources, including their study of the Charleston house with side loggias, the characteristic materials of lower Mississippi, the climatically responsive tropical British Colonial architecture, and the geometrically shaped rooms of Thomas Jefferson. The result is a newly conceived residential solution appropriate to the Florida climate, landscape, and ocean vistas.

The firm's philosophy gives careful attention to room proportion and detailing. Since the Renaissance, classical designers have expanded the body of knowledge of their field through published measured drawings that could be studied by other architects. The firm is deeply committed to sharing the knowledge they have developed in their practice, and they are currently preparing the hand-drawn illustrations for a book on frequent construction mistakes. Such contributions to the literature will assist a new generation of architects and builders.

FAIRFAX & SAMMONS

FARMLANDS
Cooperstown, New York, 2001

PRECEDING PAGES: *Lakeside facade scaled to the expansive view of Farmlands.*

ABOVE: *Formal arrival entrance.*

BELOW: *Ground-level plan.*

OPPOSITE: *Dining room with view that extends the perspective of the Zuber wallpaper.*

The American wilderness chronicled in James Fenimore Cooper's novels *The Pioneers* (1823) and *The Deerslayer* (1841) is the locale of Farmlands, a 600-acre estate overlooking Lake Oneonta. Square-edged geometric masses and simple, bold ornament create a house in tune with the rugged natural setting. Variegated local stone set in traditional load-bearing construction and a heavy natural slate roof reflect the site's unpretentious natural beauty. The palette of details maintains an aura of refinement and restraint: wood paneling with simple moldings, a stair balustrade of simple spindles, and unfluted Temple of the Winds columns. Optimal views of the lake determined the orientation of the house on its site, and each principal room takes advantage of the spectacular vista. The master bedroom suite has a commanding view of the water, with its own balcony suspended within the portico. In the formal dining room, the landscape seen through the Palladian window is echoed in the Zuber wallpaper depicting a North American hunt scene.

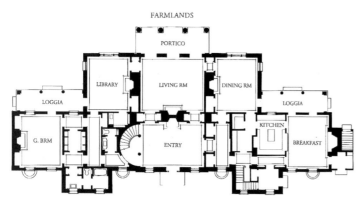

LEFT: *Pine paneled library with Palladian window.*

BELOW: *The family dining room continues the feeling of simplicity in detailing and intimacy of scale that characterizes the home's more formal public spaces.*

OPPOSITE: *The two-story entry greets visitors with a blazing fire in winter and elegant linear detailing throughout the year.*

FAIRFAX & SAMMONS

RESIDENCE
Gulf Stream, Florida, 1996

PRECEDING PAGES: *Entry facade of Gulf Stream Residence, Florida, 1996*

BELOW: *Second-story loggia on axis with the sleeping porch.*

OPPOSITE: *A Charleston-style side entry secures access to the walled garden.*

On a site adjacent to Addison Mizner's Gulfstream Country Club and its eighteenth fairway, the architects studied a variety of historic sources to produce a compatible, but not-imitative neighbor to an important work of Mizner, who established the dominant Florida style in the 1920s. Concepts from the Charleston house, tropical British Colonial architecture and lower Mississippi houses were studied to produce this inheritor of the tradition of climatically responsive classical houses. The spectacular site, overlooking the ocean, demanded the use of second-floor porches to take full advantage of the magnificent views. The owner's affection for the architecture of Thomas Jefferson inspired details reminiscent of Monticello, including Chippendale railings, oculus windows, and octagon-shaped rooms. The site was organized to save a magnificent banyan tree, which shades the verandah and second-floor porches from the heat of the setting sun.

BELOW: *Library with* faux bois *sycamore paneling.*

OPPOSITE: *Transverse hall, connecting the formal and informal living areas.*

JOHN SIMPSON
& PARTNERS

ABOVE: *Corner detail, Doric entry pavilion, Queen's Gallery, London, 2002.*

OPPOSITE: *Ceiling detail in Lord Colyton Room, Gonville and Caius College Cambridge, England, 1995.*

John Simpson is one of the most active proponents of classical and traditional architecture in Britain. He is a second-generation traditional architect, perhaps the only current architect able to claim such a heritage. Educated before World War II, his father received classical training in architecture and designed traditional styled buildings. When the younger Simpson attended the Bartlett School of Architecture and Planning in the University of London from 1972, his education was modernist tempered with a postmodern acceptance of the potential enrichment of history. In 1975, while working for Duffy, Eley, Giffoni, and Worthington, he cataloged and surveyed buildings in Covent Garden. Simpson attributes his interest in historic architecture to the lessons learned in this study. Of this experience he has said, "The conclusion to which I had come was that architecture was essentially a language for the art of building. As with any language, it was necessary to understand its intricacies and the canon of work associated with it, before you could produce lasting and significant works."[1]

After receiving his postgraduate diploma from Bartlett, he pursued his own self-education in traditional architecture by studying the work of John Soane and eighteenth- and early-nineteenth-century buildings. Of this period he says "I traveled to study and measure a number of [Soane's] surviving buildings to which I could gain access. Invariably, I was amazed at how much Soane always managed to pack into one space, for when I measured I found that the dimensions were always smaller than I expected, despite their monumentality. Also, discovering the tricks he used to create apparent symmetry out of such irregular shapes, I found especially instructive the way in which he fitted new rooms within the constraints of existing buildings."[2] Finally prepared for a career in traditional and classical architecture, Simpson established his own firm in 1980 that focuses on public and private buildings and master planning.

In 1984 and 1987 he organized exhibitions of classical work that directly influenced the Prince of Wales's decision to seek alternative schemes for the redesign of London's Paternoster Square. Simpson served as the Paternoster Square master planner from 1988 to 1992 and influenced both the removal of the 1960s squat office buildings and the reestablishment of the medieval street pattern in this historic area adjacent to St. Paul's Cathedral.

Simpson's public architecture displays his eclectic approach, which combines disparate works into intriguingly evocative forms and spaces. His most significant public works, the Queen's Gallery at Buckingham Palace and Gonville and Caius College, Cambridge, combine classical Greek details with the more recent inspiration of Soane. Always based on programmatic references, his stylistic choices are not arbitrary. For example, at Cambridge he drew inspiration for a new Fellows' Dining Hall from the cella of the Temple of Apollo Epicurius at Bassae in homage to C. R. Cockerell, the English architect whose research of Bassae is housed in Cambridge in a brilliant display of adaptability and inclusiveness of the classical language of architecture.

JOHN SIMPSON & PARTNERS

QUEEN'S GALLERY

Buckingham Palace
London, England, 2002

PRECEDING PAGES: *Street view of rear of Buckingham Palace and entry to the Queen's Gallery.*

OPPOSITE: *Doric column inspired by temples at Paestum, and frieze, sculpted by Alexander Stoddart, based on stories from the* Iliad *and the* Odyssey.

RIGHT (TOP): *Plan of main gallery floor.*

RIGHT (BOTTOM): *Redgrave lecture room inspired by the shallow domes and spare detailing of Sir John Soane.*

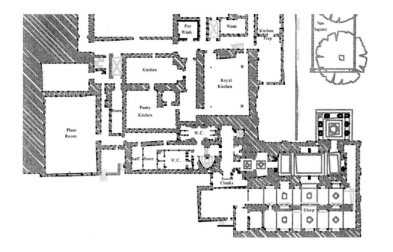

In celebration of Queen Elizabeth's Golden Jubilee, the existing Queen's Gallery was replaced and expanded more than threefold by the new project. The program called for a non-minimalist museum, and the building and its galleries are enriched with classical details, painted ornament, and period styled rooms. The sequence of referential ornament begins with the Doric portico with details developed from the Greek Doric orders added to the palace entrance in 1833. The connection of the portico to the entrance hall refers to the collision of forms on the asymmetrical Erechtheion on the Acropolis in Athens. The entrance hall is a double-height space with skylights detailed like Roman marble screens and Doric columns shaped like those primitive forms found at temples in Paestum. The internal frieze was suggested by the fifth-century-B.C. cella of the Temple of Apollo Epicurius at Bassae, Greece. The panels designed by the Scottish sculptor Alexander Stoddart depict scenes from the *Iliad* and the *Odyssey*. Marking the internal entry to the museum are two life-size genies sculpted by Stoddart from images inspired by a description of the Hall of Alcinous in the *Odyssey*. The new galleries draw inspiration from nineteenth-century English architects John Nash and John Soane.

BELOW: *The Nash Gallery is inserted within the walls of a John Nash pavilion, the interiors of which had been obliterated by earlier renovations. John Simpson sought inspiration for the new beamed and bracketed ceiling from various works by Nash. The ceiling beams provide walkways for technicians working on the elaborate lighting system.*

OPPOSITE: *The Pennethorne Gallery houses changing exhibitions of paintings and art objects from the Royal Collection. The three-part ceiling with top lighting is inspired by concepts from both Nash and Soane. The walls are covered with an Isle of Bute woolen fabric and the deep base is made of polished black marble.*

GONVILLE AND CAIUS COLLEGE

Cambridge, England, 1995

OPPOSITE: *The new Lord Colyton Room developed from a surviving watercolor of Soane's original 1792 design.*

BELOW (LEFT): *New fireplace surround, mirror, and wall sconces in the Lord Colyton Room reflect the reserved linearity of Soane's detailing.*

BELOW (RIGHT): *Plan of principal rooms.*

In 1988 Gonville and Caius College acquired the University Library designed by C. R. Cockerell between 1837 and 1840. A limited competition for remodeling the building was won in 1993 by Simpson. The remodeling resulted in a series of magnificent rooms owing their appearance to the inspiration of John Soane and Cockerell. A Soane dining hall of 1792 that had been destroyed by later alterations served as the starting point for a new Fellows' Reading Room, renamed the Lord Colyton Room. Drawing upon a surviving Soane rendering of the former dining hall, details for the new Colyton Room developed in keeping with the original. In the adjacent Fellows' Dining Room, Simpson looked to the career of Cockerell for inspiration, as an homage to the architect of the original University Library. The detailing references the important archaeological discoveries made by Cockerell in 1810 and 1811 at the Temple of Apollo Epicurius at Bassae, Greece. The new dining room references the temple's cella, with its distinctive spur walls with attached Ionic columns, polychromatic detailing, and, most significantly, the re-creation of what was believed to be the first found Corinthian column.

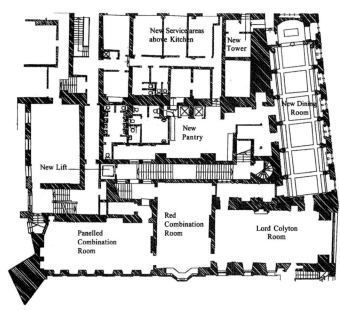

BELOW: *The Bassae frieze was obtained by Cockerell for the British museum and was reproduced here from plaster casts. The bold coloration is inspired by the original coloration of Greek temples.*

OPPOSITE: *Fellows' dining room at Caius College with the frieze, partly engaged Ionic Columns, and Corinthian column developed through study of the Temple of Apollo Epicurius, Bassae. The forty-four foot long dining table is of walnut with bronze mounts and inlaid with ebonized wood anthemion ornament. The chairs are of sycamore and bronze, and derive from chairs depicted on Greek vases.*

FERGUSON & SHAMAMIAN
ARCHITECTS, LLP

ABOVE AND OPPOSITE: *Residential renovation focused on new mantel and surround with column details drawn from the Temple of Apollo at Bassae. Ahmad Suleiman fabricated the scagliola marble. The interior designer was Bunny Williams.*

Mark Ferguson and Oscar Shamamian founded their firm in 1988 on a shared enthusiasm for the formal classical and regional traditional details that characterize the firm's work. Their residential designs in Palm Beach draw inspiration from the 1920s Florida style of Addison Mizner; while in California, Spanish baroque provides sources for contextual material and detailing; and in northeastern ocean communities, the romantic massing of nineteenth-century shingle-style houses provides a strong image for their new designs.

Both partners received modern educations—Ferguson at Princeton and Shamamian at Columbia—but the period of their education in the early 1980s was shaped by the more philosophically open period of postmodernism. Although classical design was actively discouraged in school, Ferguson recalls, "Postmodernist theory and criticism infused my undergraduate education. The rejection of avant-garde modernism and a return to history revived the exploration of figurative design and my interest in architectural traditions and regionalism." The detailed knowledge Ferguson needed to create excellent classical and traditional design was, by necessity, self-taught. He launched his personal education with the study of *The American Vignola*, by William R. Ware, and, for details, consulted the *Fragments D'Architecture Antique* by H. D'Espouy and the *Edifices de Rome Moderne* by Paul Letarouilly.

Shamamian first discovered his interest in classical design while working part-time as a photo researcher for Robert A. M. Stern's book project *New York 1900*. While gathering the images of projects by turn-of-the-century American classical architects such as McKim, Mead & White, and Delano & Aldrich, he discovered a profound fascination that modern design had failed to inspire. He was additionally inspired by his surroundings at Columbia, whose campus plan and notable Low Library had been designed by McKim, Mead & White. He brought this new interest in historical reference to his studio projects, but found no support for them in the milieu of the Columbia graduate studio. The lack of tolerance for historical design was particularly surprising considering the historic campus that surrounded the architecture students as well as the university's celebrated Avery Library, the most significant architectural collection in America. Like Ferguson, Shamamian found that he would have to teach himself in order to develop his understanding of traditional and classical architecture. However, he did find support for his interests in art and architecture history courses and in the office of Stern, a sympathetic mentor.

Ferguson and Shamamian met at the renowned interior design firm of Parish-Hadley Associates, which assisted Jacqueline Kennedy in the decoration of the White House and also the personal homes of the president and his wife. Both Ferguson and Shamamian had their first classical and traditional design opportunities in the early 1980s—Ferguson with an addition to a small fieldstone cottage originally designed by Ernest Flagg, and Shamamian with the renovation of a 1920s Georgian mansion in Washington, D.C.

Their fifty-person firm, located in New York City, has built projects throughout the United States. Although residential architecture from country estates to apartments is their principal focus, the firm also designs garden structures and creates master plans for resort communities and country clubs. Their work is characterized by a relationship with local building traditions, landscape and regional environment, a passion for excellent detailing, use of fine materials, and exceptional workmanship. The firm has received numerous awards, most recently the 2003 Arthur Ross Award for Residential Architecture and Town Planning from the Institute of Classical Architecture and Classical America.

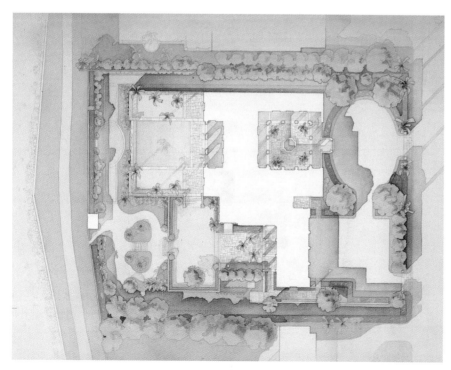

Located on the edge of Lake Worth, the 12,000 square-foot residence shares a kinship with the family of designs inspired by the Italian Renaissance and F. Burrall Hoffman, the locally revered architect of Vizcaya in Miami. The plan arranges the house in five layers along an axis leading from the public elliptical court surrounded by an eight-foot-tall hedge, through a projecting entrance portico, into an atrium with a fountain, and finally into the house proper. Upon entering the living room, the visitor's eye is drawn through to the loggia, pool, gardens, and the dramatic view across Lake Worth. The double-height groin vaulted living room has dark stained oak wainscot interrupted by a large carved stone mantel inspired in scale and feeling by those found in Florentine Renaissance villas. The Florida-style interpretation of the Renaissance forms is conveyed though load-bearing masonry with stucco walls, cast stone detailing with the appearance of travertine, extended cypress rafter-tails, and the clay barrel tile roof.

LEFT: *The wrought-iron stair railing was inspired by the detailing found in early Palm Beach residences. The interior designer was The John Cottrell Company.*

BELOW: *Architect's drawing for the cast-stone fireplace surround fabricated by Ahmad Suleiman.*

OPPOSITE: *The mantelpiece, vaulting, Ionic corbels and paneled walls convey the feeling of a sixteenth-century Florentine interior.*

FERGUSON & SHAMAMIAN ARCHITECTS, LLP

RESIDENCE

Bridgewater, Connecticut
Main House, Pool House, Barn/Greenhouse, Grounds, 1993
Loggia and Carriage House, 2001

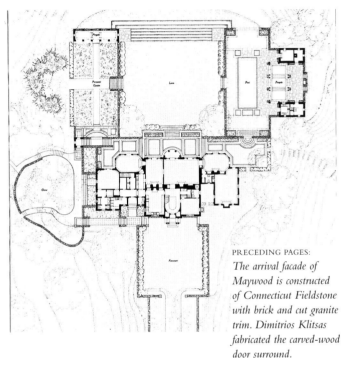

PRECEDING PAGES:
The arrival facade of Maywood is constructed of Connecticut Fieldstone with brick and cut granite trim. Dimitrios Klitsas fabricated the carved-wood door surround.

ABOVE AND OPPOSITE:
Garden facade.

In 1988, work at this site began with an octagonal library addition to the existing neocolonial house. The quality of the library was superior to the existing house, so the owner requested a new 10,000-square-foot, three-bedroom addition replacing the existing house. The rural site and the owner's love of gardening suggested a Georgian-influenced design. The original faceted library is balanced on the opposite side of the main two-story block with a similarly shaped room. The quiet facade is composed of gray fieldstone, contrasting red brick quoins and jack arches, and white painted mahogany trim. The garden facade is entirely rendered in white painted mahogany cut to simulate stone details. Similar detailing occurs in the two-story entry stair hall with its plaster walls articulated as ashlar masonry blocks and its wood plank floor painted to resemble marble. The loggia and carriage house, added in 2001, frame a Giverney-style garden whose gentle patterns can be viewed from the balcony of the raised loggia. The large arched windows in the loggia are motorized and can be lowered into the rusticated base to open the building to views and breezes.

LEFT: *Loggia interior with eleven-foot-tall motorized windows, 2001. Below: Pool house, 1993.*

OPPOSITE: *Loggia viewed from the garden.*

LEFT: *Sitting room with shallow saucer dome inspired by Sir John Soane.*

BELOW: *Dining room interior design by Bunny Williams. Architect-designed Chinoiserie paneling and hand-painted Chinese wallpaper by John Roselli.*

OPPOSITE: *The architects explored the American tradition of faux materials with simulated ashlar masonry block walls of plaster and marbleized wood flooring.*

ALLAN GREENBERG
ARCHITECT

ABOVE: *Main entrance to 65,000-square-foot Gore Hall at the University of Delaware.*

OPPOSITE: *Beechwoods entrance with eighteenth-century American detailing.*

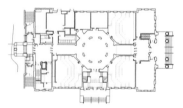

Allan Greenberg is an accomplished architect, historian, and writer whose approach to architecture is rooted in the relationship between politics and aesthetics. His fascination with eighteenth- and nineteenth-century American architecture is related to their genesis in the American Revolution and their architects' commitment to expressing American democratic ideals in architectural form. He has eloquently recorded his thoughts in both his article "The Architecture of Democracy" and his book, *George Washington Architect*.[1]

Greenberg's background differs from other architects who appear to share his sensibilities—he was trained in both classicism and modernism, and sees no contradiction in admiring the architecture of Jefferson and Lutyens and that of modern masters like Le Corbusier and Alvar Aalto, or in his experience working with Jørn Utzon during the design phase of the Sydney Opera House. Greenberg regards himself as a modern architect, not a traditionalist, who is committed to a renaissance of the political idealism that created the American Revolution and the architecture of that period.

Greenberg was born in Johannesburg, South Africa, and his architectural education at the University of Witwatersrand included drawing the historic models of classical and gothic architecture from memory.[2] He came to the United States to study under Paul Rudolph at Yale, where he received his master of architecture degree in 1965. His architecture is both exquisitely detailed and employs the most current construction techniques. On this topic he wrote, "Though Modernism claims to have brought technology to architecture, in fact it had been fully absorbed into the fabric of American classical architecture before the end of the 19th century. Classical architecture forged a new synthesis between the building industry and technology that revolutionized both the fabrication of materials and construction technology; it has always responded to the needs of architecture, current and future, at the same time reinterpreting the past and drawing it into the present."[3]

In 1972, Greenberg established his firm which currently has offices in New York City, Washington, D.C., and Greenwich, Connecticut. Architects trained at many of the major architecture schools have worked for his firm. Because these schools do not prepare their students to work in classical design, his office provided an apprenticeship to many young architects and teachers. Today classical design is taught at the University of Notre Dame, where Greenberg's son Peter trained, and the University of Miami under Elizabeth Plater-Zyberk, one of Greenberg's students when he taught at Yale.

Greenberg's first project involved an Aalto-inspired addition in 1973 to the State Library and Supreme Court Building in Hartford, Connecticut, designed by Donn Barber in 1908. After this initial exposure to working in a historic context, his approach quickly transformed to one that strives to reconnect American architecture and urbanism to its fundamental root in the late colonial and Federal periods. His work includes public, commercial, university, and institutional buildings as well as residences.

In addition to running his architectural practice, Greenberg has taught at Yale University's architecture and law schools, the University of Pennsylvania, and the Division of Historic Preservation at Columbia University.

ALLAN GREENBERG ARCHITECT

UNIVERSITY OF DELAWARE
Gore Hall and Dupont Hall
Newark, Delaware, 1998 and 2002

DUPONT HALL LABORATORY EXPANSION
UNIVERSITY OF DELAWARE
NEWARK, DELAWARE
ALLAN GREENBERG ARCHITECT, LLC

0 4   16   32 feet

PRECEDING PAGES: *Du Pont Hall faces Gore Hall (not shown) across The Mall at the University of Delaware.*

LEFT (TOP): *Main floor plan of Du Pont Hall.*

BOTTOM (LEFT): *Entrance portico of Du Pont Hall, the new College of Engineering, named in honor of the early benefactor Pierre S. du Pont.*

BELOW (RIGHT): *Main floor plan of Gore Hall.*

OPPOSITE: *Entrance lobby of Du Pont Hall.*

Gore Hall and Dupont Hall complement the historic character of the University of Delaware by completing the edges of the central quadrangle, called the Mall. Both buildings are detailed in the same materials, scale, and rhythm of window opening to wall mass as their neighbors on the Mall, further strengthening the Georgian character of Day and Klauder's original campus plan. The new buildings' entry porticoes reflect the civic formality of campus architecture established by Memorial Hall. Gore Hall serves as a classroom building approached from two equally important sides of the campus, responding with a respectful temple facade on the Mall and a lower keyed entrance from the opposite side. The building's entry axis focuses on a central three-story rotunda that allows visitors immediate orientation. Dupont Hall completes the original campus master plan and adds to the character of the Mall with its own unique pedimented porch. Interior classical detailing is limited to the entrance lobby with the remainder of the building dedicated to highly technical classroom and laboratory spaces.

ALLAN GREENBERG ARCHITECT

HUCKLEBERRY HOUSE, 1982–1985

Garden Pavilion and Garden
Connecticut, 1989–1990

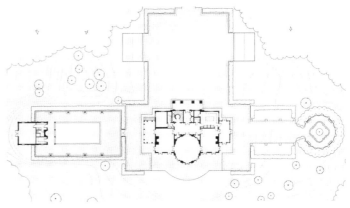

As the garden facade clearly reads, the focus of the house was a two-story domed ballroom. The low stepped dome and project- ing curved room bring the work of Benjamin Latrobe to mind. Ease of circulation during frequent social events directed the creation of en-suite connection between the main public rooms. The house is organized along two principal axes that cross in the broad rectangular hall. The pedimented main entry opens on axis to the ballroom, designating its primary position within the com- position. The lateral axis extends from a garden event on one end to a pool pavilion on the other. Within the house the axis passes through the side of the rooms, but pure symmetry of design is maintained in each case by matching French doors to either side of the central fireplaces. On one side of the axis the exterior room is an open porch and on the other an enclosed sunroom.

147

PRECEDING PAGES: *A Roman Doric temple enhances the scale of the carefully detailed small house.*

BELOW (LEFT): *The rear porch is detailed like a single story model of George Washington's Mount Vernon.*

BELOW (RIGHT): *Main floor plan.*

OPPOSITE: *Circular entrance hall (see page 8).*

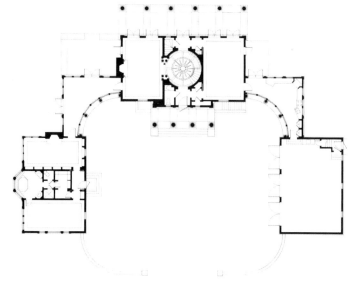

This residence combines the client's interest in Palladio and the architect's enthusiasm for eighteenth-century American architecture. The Palladian five-part plan of the central house symmetrically connected by glazed hyphens to outbuildings is rendered in American materials of stained shingles and wood detailing. The carefully detailed Doric temple face leads to the wood entry wall detailed with rusticated joints as if it were made of stone. This eighteenth-century device of elevating the status of a lesser material is well known to the architect from the research for his recent *George Washington Architect*. The entry door surround developed from an eighteenth-century precedent as well. The house revolves around a centered circular stair hall with flooring detailed as a compass rose.

PORPHYRIOS
ASSOCIATES

Demetri Porphyrios has an international reputation as an architect and theorist. His design approach is informed by his humanist philosophy: "Experience and common sense tell us that what makes good architecture possible is the dialogue between the craft of building and the great humanist theme of commodity, firmness, and delight: a design philosophy which aims at balancing the requirements of the brief (commodity) with the necessities of good construction (firmness) and the expectations of civility and aesthetics (delight). This has been the guiding design philosophy of our practice and it is in that sense that our buildings speak of tradition as that which endures." Porphyrios had extensive academic training at Princeton University including two master's degrees, in architecture (1974) and the arts (1975), and a doctorate in architecture (1982). Like other architects of his generation, however, he is self-taught in classical design. Of his education he says, "My formal training at Princeton was a Corbusian modernism. Through my theory classes I was introduced to French eighteenth- and nineteenth-century classicism as well as the Italian Renaissance. My interest in classical antiquity and the robust construction of classical and traditional buildings generally grew through my first-hand knowledge of classical buildings." The architects he considers most influential on his career— Christian and Theophilos Hansen, Leo von Klenze, Sigurd Lewerentz, and Alvar Aalto—help explain, in part, his inventive combination of traditional, classical, and modern design. "The classical," he says, "reaches across culture and time, and taking the risk of anachronism, it heals the estrangement which humanism constantly faces: the classical is certainly the enduring and timeless. But this timelessness always takes the form of modernity; that is, it takes the form of the relevance of tradition."

Porphyrios has explored his design philosophy through building, teaching, and writing. He has held the Jefferson professorship at the University of Virginia and the Davenport and Bishop professorship at Yale University. He received an Honorary Doctorate from the University of Notre Dame. His publications include *Sources of Modern Eclecticism* (1982), *Classicism is Not a Style* (1982), *On the Methodology of Architectural History* (1984), *Building and Architecture* (1984), *Classical Architecture* (1993), and numerous essays. The work of his firm has been presented in two monographs in 1993 and 1999.

In 1985, Porphyrios founded his London office and has completed projects that include public and private architecture, interior design, planning, and urban design. His twenty-five-person firm has received numerous international awards including the European Award for the Reconstruction of the City in 1992 for Belvedere Village, Ascot, and in 1998 for the town of Pitiousa, Spetses; the Regional Award for Best Office Building from the British Council for Offices Awards in 1999 for Three Brindleyplace, Birmingham; the MIPIM Residential Development Award in 1997 for the town of Pitiousa, Spetses; and recognition as a Royal Fine Art Commission Building of the Year Award finalist in 1997 for the New Grove Quadrangle, Magdalen College, Oxford. He is a member of CABE (Committee for Architecture and the Built Environment in England) and of Europa Nostra. In recognition of his work as an architect, theorist, and educator, he was selected for the 2004 Driehaus Prize.

TOP: *Main entrance.*

BOTTOM: *Ground level plan.*

OPPOSITE: *View of the arrival facade*

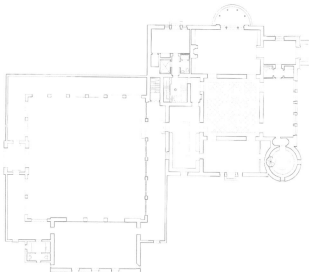

The Duncan Galleries serves as both a private house and gallery for the display of modern abstract sculpture. The classical detailing combined with the modernist use of stainless steel reflects the eclectic taste of a client who enjoys both hand-woven baskets and machine-finished abstract pieces. Nebraska's surreal expanse of flat earth and endless sky influenced the architect's decisions. The walls of Indiana limestone tie the design to the earth while the stainless steel columns and balconies create dreamlike versions of classical details. The sense of the fantastic extends into the square grid landscape punctuated at intersection points and at the ends of axes with gigantic sculptures. The principal exhibition space and entertaining rooms open to the central glazed atrium.

TOP: *Library.*

BOTTOM: *Glazed atrium exhibition area with figure on horse— "Le Cheval Et La Mariee" by Niki de Saint Phalle, 1963–97.*

OPPOSITE: *Side garden.*

FOLLOWING PAGES: *Arrival view of the gallery across the Nebraska land-scape with the sculpture "Eileen" by Philip Grausman, 1999.*

PORPHYRIOS ASSOCIATES

NEW GROVE QUADRANGLE AUDITORIUM

Magdalen College, Oxford, England, 1998

Beginning in 1994, Porphyrios Associates designed a new quadrangle for Magdalen College, Oxford, which included residential buildings and a 150-seat auditorium and exhibition gallery. Carefully conceived architectural detailing distinguishes the private and public areas of the complex. The housing is detailed in ashlar Ketton stone with Tudor arches, and crenellations with a scale and massing that reflect the historic character of Oxford's colleges. The auditorium is detailed in simplified, almost primitive, classical pilasters and gabled roof that subtly mark it as the public building in the complex.

PORPHYRIOS ASSOCIATES

THREE BRINDLEYPLACE
OFFICE BUILDING

Birmingham, England, 1998

BELOW: *Doric colonnade with interlocking arches.*

RIGHT: *Ground floor plan.*

OPPOSITE: *View from the square.*

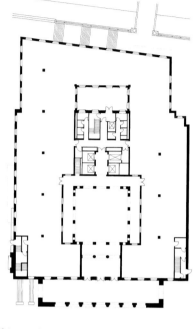

Within a pioneering master-planned, mixed-use development in Birmingham, Three Brindleyplace provides the identifying focus for a renewed area of the city. The red brick walls and classical details of the 120,000-square-foot office building contrast with the material palette of its modernist neighbors. The building's approximately 164-foot-tall Italianate clock tower answered the client's request for a landmark sign for the development as a whole. The building steps down from seven stories on the urban square to a height of three stories on the canal side in response to the changing scale of its surroundings. Upon entering the building, the visitor's feeling of scale is modulated by an exterior double-height arcade and the lofty foyer at the main entrance, which then opens onto a dramatic seven-story glazed atrium.

The building is a dialogue between modern and classical design. Two coordinated structural systems are employed—an internal steel frame and an external masonry bearing wall system, a dual system employed by the first Chicago skyscrapers. The modern tall building truthfully expresses both the masonry detailing of flat and pointed arches and the post and beam system of the steel frame. The detailing is also carefully orchestrated to present the structural nature of the classical orders and the decorative relief provided by classical anthemia, reeds, roundels and acroteria.

LEFT: *Architectural model of the Atrium.*

OPPOSITE: *View of atrium from entrance foyer.*

HARRISON DESIGN
ASSOCIATES

ABOVE: *Hand-forged iron and bronze balustrade designed by the late Jacques Brunet of Paris, former head of the French Iron Workers' Guild. Residence, Atlanta, Georgia, 2002.*

OPPOSITE: *Indiana limestone columns and details of entry porch, Residence, Atlanta, Georgia, 2003.*

Bill Harrison founded his design firm in 1991, and his partner, Greg Palmer, joined the firm in 1995. Harrison and Palmer share a vision of architecture that is both modern and traditional. The aesthetic preferences of the two architects are not limited to a particular period or style, but encompass all that fall within the realm of humanist architecture. They also share a belief that architects of all periods have employed the latest technology in their buildings, and excellence in fundamental construction and detailing characterizes their work. Both Harrison and Palmer have extensive experience in construction as well as design.

Bill Harrison received his architectural training in the modernist program at the Georgia Institute of Technology. The head of the school in the 1960s, Paul M. Heffernan, had won the Paris Prize and studied at the Ecole des Beaux-Arts from 1935 to 1938, but he was equally influenced by the German Bauhaus. His numerous buildings on the Georgia Tech campus, including the architecture building, demonstrated an easy alliance between beaux-arts planning and superficial Bauhaus detailing. Heffernan shared this respect for history, both distant and recent, with his design students. Influenced by Heffernan's eclectic interests, after leaving Georgia Tech, Harrison embarked on a five-year self-directed study tour of world architecture that took him through Europe and North and South America. He worked with various architects during his travels and recorded details that he would later use in the work of his firm.

Greg Palmer studied architecture at the Southern Technical Institute, near Atlanta. Although this program was based in modernism, the faculty allowed students to explore the use of traditional styles in their designs. Palmer's father and grandfather are general contractors, and he grew up working on construction sites. This extensive practical knowledge, combined with his interest in historic architecture, contribute to the firm's well-crafted buildings, made with authentic period details incorporating both indigenous and exotic materials. In their efforts to provide the highest quality construction, the firm often uses pre-stressed concrete floor systems, which allow them to select heavier flooring materials like marble and granite and also allows their clients the freedom to place heavy decorative objects at their discretion throughout their homes. This floor system was developed for commercial construction, but the benefits in span and load capacity make it ideal for fine residential construction as well.

The firm's philosophy focuses on fulfilling the architectural desires of their clients. Harrison says, "It is our goal for our homes to be a reflection of our clients' preferences and style. Our task is to take our clients' dreams and through collaboration make them better than they could have possibly imagined." Harrison Design Associates has offices in Atlanta, Georgia, and Santa Barbara, California. The firm's work includes residential, ecclesiastical, commercial, and community design. They have completed projects throughout the United States, the Caribbean, the Middle East, and the Far East.

RESIDENCE

Atlanta, Georgia, 2003

PRECEDING PAGES: *Garden elevation. Residence, Atlanta, Georgia, 2003.*

TOP (LEFT): *Front elevation and arrival court.*

BOTTOM (LEFT): *Dining room.*

BOTTOM (RIGHT): *Ground floor plan.*

OPPOSITE: *Two-story entry foyer with spiral stair that floats free on one side.*

The house's site is characteristic of the dramatic beauty of Atlanta's hilly wooded landscape. Old trees encouraged a design that conveyed a sense of history. The Georgian-inspired residence develops a subtle hierarchy to focus attention on the main entrance. The building uses Flemish bond brick throughout, but the main block of the five-part composition has limestone quoins and carved plaques distinguishing it from the apparently later outbuildings connected by hyphens, which feature brick detailed quoins. The entry porch is detailed with reserved twelve-foot Doric limestone columns and a curving entablature. To answer the owners' love of entertaining, the house was designed with open arches rather than doors to encourage free movement throughout the formal spaces into the covered porches, formal gardens, and pool area.

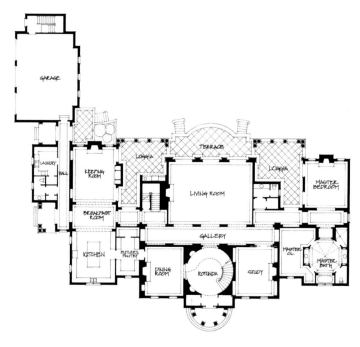

ABOVE: *Library with paneled walls and egg and dart molding of American white pine resawn from 150-year-old timbers salvaged from demolished buildings.*

RIGHT: *View of gallery opening to formal living room. The fireplace is a reproduction of the Coadestone parlor mantle of the Tayloe (Octagon) House, Washington, D.C. designed by Dr. William Thornton, original architect of the U.S. Capitol.*

HARRISON DESIGN ASSOCIATES

RESIDENCE
Atlanta, Georgia, 2002

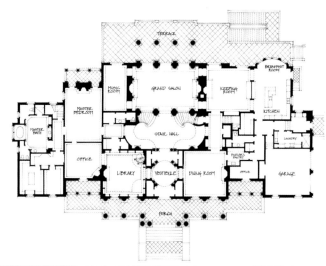

PRECEDING PAGES: *The American Beaux-arts inspired residence is fully detailed in Indiana limestone and includes solid-shaft twenty-seven-foot fluted Corinthian columns. The ten-foot-tall entry doors are reclaimed from a French chateau.*

LEFT (TOP): *Entry level plan.*

LEFT (BOTTOM): *Stair hall detailed with Giallo Siena marble from Italy.*

OPPOSITE: *View from stair hall into entry vestibule through solid Rouge de Roi columns with gilded Ionic capitals.*

The owner requested the finest materials for this 28,000-square-foot house, which included Indiana and Texas limestone, Giallo Siena and Rouge de Roi marbles, wrought iron from France, crotch mahoghany, burl cherry, and burl walnut. The entry facade's 27-foot Corinthian columns are made of single shafts of Indiana limestone that required three years to quarry and sculpt. Jacques Brunet of Paris, former head of the French Iron Worker's Guild, designed and shaped wrought iron with bronze embellishments for the handrails and openwork bronze doors. George Vanderbilt's favorite room at the Biltmore House in Asheville, his art library, inspired the design for the two-story library with spiral stair and balustrade. The house's formal spaces include a two-story salon, music room, dining room, and library. The entertainment spaces on the terrace level include a wine cellar and tasting room, home theater, shooting gallery, billiard room and pub, and swimming pool.

LEFT: *Wine cellar and tasting room with structural vaulting and walls of Texas limestone. Cold water lines in the walls stabilize the temperature of the wine and warm water lines beneath the travertine floor provide radiant heating.*

BELOW (LEFT): *Dining room with antique fireplace surround from Italy.*

BELOW (RIGHT): *View of the dining room from the vestibule.*

OPPOSITE: *The grand salon with a matched pair of monumental fireplace surrounds inspired by a fireplace observed by the client at the Louvre.*

BELOW: *Spiral stair in library patterned after George Vanderbilt's library at Biltmore House. The room is detailed with walnut paneling and burl walnut veneers.*

OPPOSITE: *The antique fireplace front was enlarged to fit the scale of the two-story library.*

LEFT (TOP): *Triple arched doors of hand wrought iron with bronze details designed by the late Jacques Brunet of Paris. A gate in France commissioned by Napoleon inspired Brunet's design.*

LEFT (BOTTOM): *Early-French-Renaissance-style exterior loggia fireplace made of Indiana limestone.*

RIGHT: *Rear portico overlooking ground floor vaulted exterior living space and swimming pool.*

MICHAEL G. IMBER
ARCHITECT

ABOVE AND OPPOSITE: *Daniell Residence, San Antonio, Texas, 2000. The carved stone lintel above the entry and other decorative details are made of the local Leuders limestone.*

Michael G. Imber is the principal of a ten-person firm in San Antonio, Texas. The firm is best known for the regional vernacular character of its work, but projects have also included carefully proportioned and detailed classical work, most significantly those developed from the Spanish colonial heritage of Texas and Mexico. This influence ranges from the simple smooth curves of the hacienda to the crisply carved decoration of the proposed chapel of Our Lady of Corpus Christi in South Texas.

Imber's studies at Texas Tech University explored the varied regional traditions of Texas vernacular architecture. Through apprenticeship with Shope-Reno-Wharton in Connecticut and Allan Greenberg in Washington, D.C., he learned the principles of the new American traditionalism as well as high-style classical design. A native Texan, Imber returned home to found a firm whose work would be characterized by the expression of regional colloquialisms as developed through the sophistication of a well-trained classicist. All the members of Imber's firm have expertise in both vernacular and high-style design.

This firm first studies the specific traditions and cultural influences of the site and then creates a fitting, measured classical response. Regional influences on Texas's architectural character, from Kentucky migrants settling in east Texas, Germans in the Hill Country, and Spanish immigrants predominating in the southwest region, to the revival of twentieth-century classical suburban traditions, have contributed to the firm's broad portfolio of work. Decisions as wide ranging as molding profiles and hardware to building material and massing are developed from investigation of these local traditions. They have employed this regionally responsive approach in more recent work in California, Colorado, and Florida.

The firm selects materials that express regional connectedness. The most characteristic materials used in their Texas architecture are the beautiful Hill Country limestone and the earth and lime mass walls evocative of the Spanish southwest. Their material choices may verify the appropriateness of the existing vernacular, but they are also environmentally conscious and of the highest technological innovation. The mass stuccoed walls that functioned so well historically to maintain a cool interior in a desert climate are now constructed with Autoclaved Aerated Concrete, a green building material more commonly found in Europe than America. Modernists often chide traditionalists for both the use of modern materials and yet again for the avoidance of nontraditional materials and methods. The appropriateness of Imber's work in a severe climatic region demonstrates the continued wisdom of the old and the new regional vernacular.

PALACIO ÑECA

Fort Worth, Texas, 2004

The Palacio Ñeca reflects a Spanish and Italian design heritage with refined stucco walls that contrast effectively with the rugged landscape of the Texas Hill Country. The house is sited at the end of a sinuous driveway that winds up to a wooded limestone hilltop. From here, glimpses of terraced gardens, fountains, and the west facade of the house are seen at an angle revealing the villa's grand scale. The house is anchored to its site with a heavily rusticated Texas limestone base and arches modeled after the Palazzo Pitti in Florence. A seventeenth-century-inspired fountain complements the formal baroque south facade also composed of limestone and plaster. A pair of impressively heavy entry doors lead to a delicately scaled entry foyer that opens to a great rotunda. This multistory space is articulated by levels of colonnaded arcades and crowned by attic niches. The elaborate dining room is embellished with Mudejar-style carved wood wall and ceiling panels. Located off the main gallery, the grand stair with marble winding steps has a ceiling of stained glass that throws colored light into the space. At the heart of the villa, the principle two-story room, with its large arched steel windows, has dramatic views of the west garden terraces, pool and pavilions, and the surrounding Hill Country.

LEFT (TOP): *Watercolor study of the library by Stefan Molina.*

LEFT (BOTTOM): *Ground floor plan. Computer generated rendering in the style of a Beaux-arts watercolor by Roberto Trevino.*

OPPOSITE: *Principal entry study in watercolor by Michael Imber and Stefan Molina.*

MICHAEL G. IMBER, ARCHITECT

INVERNESS GATEHOUSE AND PARK PAVILION

San Antonio, Texas, 2002

The development of Inverness transformed an old family ranch that had been engulfed by urban growth into an upscale residential area in San Antonio. A gatehouse accommodating an office marks the development's formal entry with a pavilion of cut stone and randomly coursed Texas Leuders limestone covered by a slate roof. On the arrival side, the arched windows and iron gates hint at the functions of the gatehouse. Facing the neighborhood, the gatehouse creates a shared community pavilion, with an open loggia that acts as the anchor of a series of walking paths. This contrast of rough coursed field stone with cut limestone is analogous to the elegant development and its natural setting of mottled oaks and open grassy pastures.

Within the development, the Park Pavilion anchors the neighborhood and acts as the gateway to a natural greenbelt with walking trails. Framed by a crescent drive and a low stone ha-ha that serves as the bank of a creek bed, an open lawn leads to the pavilion, which is joined by a low stone wall and pergola. Each was built around a cut stone column wrapped by a circular wooden bench, and capped by a stone urn at rooftop. Again the contrast of the formal and the natural takes place, as the pergola overlooks a lower court framed by a set of stone stairs descending to a grotto. A stone exedra opens in the base of the pavilion and is the ceremonial source of a calm pool facing an open green space, which runs along an old creek canyon that now serves as flood control for the area. The exedra is the trailhead of a greenbelt, forming a connection with the community.

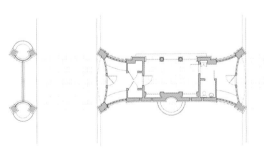

PRECEDING PAGES: *Arrival face of the Inverness Gatehouse.*

ABOVE: *Community side of the gatehouse with covered loggia and garden.*

RIGHT: *Park Pavilion on the grotto side with pool.*

MICHAEL G. IMBER, ARCHITECT

DANIELL HOUSE

San Antonio, Texas, 2000

PRECEDING PAGES: *Octagonal shaped entry court with cobblestone and Mexican brick pavement. The triple arched doors form an axis that terminates with the pool pavilion.*

LEFT (TOP): *Living room with paneled mahogany walls and flat barrel vault.*

LEFT (BOTTOM): *Main floor plan and second floor insert.*

OPPOSITE: *View from the dining room through the living room to the carved limestone columns at the entry.*

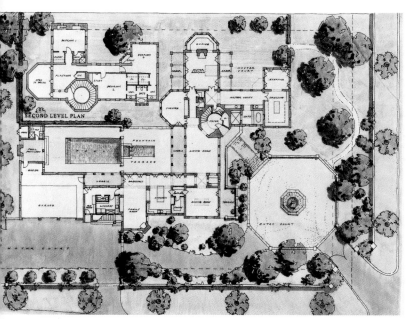

Designed in the Italian Revival Style of the 1920's, white plaster, cream Texas limestone, and a clay barrel tile roof embody the character of the historic Mediterranean homes characteristic of the surrounding neighborhood. An existing stone wall and iron gate from an earlier farm estate lend a sense of history to the property. They were reused as part of the formal entry court where a brick and stone drive surround a large central fountain. The house forms an "s" around this entry point in order to afford the best orientation and exposure for the interior spaces. On axis with the existing gate, the octagonal stair tower anchors the entry court and divides the public and private spaces of the house.

The Mediterranean tradition of balancing interior and exterior living spaces characterizes the design of the house. Entering the living room through a pair of stone columns, the room opens on one side to the entry court through three arched windows and to a covered loggia on a private pool terrace on the other. Passing through a sky-lighted corridor, the mahogany paneled dining room opens to a small dining terrace on the entry court. The pool terrace is anchored on the far end by a pavilion with outdoor fireplace. A formal cut stone loggia anchors the other end of the pool at the house and provides a covered seating area off the living room. The layout of the house allows for courts or gardens off each of the main living spaces, including a trellis covered sitting area off the master bedroom and a "secret garden" off the master bath and the exercise room.

BELOW: *The three arched openings on the entry court initiate an axis that crosses the living room and opens to this exterior loggia with attached columns.*

OPPOSITE: *The exterior loggia faces the triple arched openings of the pool pavilion.*

ROBERT A. M. STERN
ARCHITECTS

One of the world's leading architects, Robert A. M. Stern enjoys a professional recognition that stems from his numerous activities as an architect, writer, teacher, and lecturer. In 1986, his humor and insight reached a vast audience through his eight-part documentary television series on the Public Broadcasting System titled *Pride of Place: Building the American Dream*, which brought into America's living rooms a new understanding and respect for architecture.

Stern received his master's degree in architecture from Yale University in 1965 and opened his first practice in 1969. His 150-person firm is now organized with partners and associate partners, but he continues to direct the design of each project. Along with Michael Graves and Robert Venturi, he initiated the postmodernism movement, which opened a dialogue around the fundamental place of history in an architect's education and, consequently, in the practice of architecture. Although Venturi and Graves each worked to increase the expressive quality of modern architecture, only Stern allowed his work to explore the noncanonical realm of historic inspiration. Stern's firm does not have a single stylistic expression, but draws an appropriate expression from the needs and context of each program. Stern states:

I am not interested in a personal style or being part of a singular stylistic movement. I am interested in the suggestive possibilities of the place. I want my buildings to be portraits of the places where they are built. For this reason I am less interested in architecture as the representation of innovative genius and more interested in architecture as the act of contextual invention.[1]

For over thirty years Robert Stern has demonstrated the richness of an eclectic approach to design. His willingness to explore historic sources brings greater meaning to architecture through connections of the present with the past. His continuing interest in the shingle style derives from its appropriateness as an American form balancing rough texture with refined massing and detail. His acknowledgment that public architecture demands an expressive scale, order, and symbolism enriches such buildings as libraries and museums with the readable ornament that reminds the citizenry of their heritage. In his many "goodtime places" produced for the Walt Disney Company, he draws upon the expressive power of humor.

Stern has served as teacher and mentor for students at Columbia and Yale and has inspired scores of other students and professionals through the example of his work. From 1984 to 1988 he was the first director of Columbia's Temple Hoyne Buell Center for the Study of American Architecture and is now the J. M. Hoppin Professor of Architecture and Dean of Yale School of Architecture. He has broadened the understanding of American architecture through the numerous books that he has authored or co-authored; and eleven books have been published on the work of his firm. His 1975 biography of George Howe was an early exploration of a traditional architect whose later work produced an American face for the international style. Stern's career mirrored Howe's, but in reverse. As Stern matured in thinking and experience, his work displayed an increasingly diverse and poetic production, moving away from the earlier simple abstractions that marked his youthful creations.

ROBERT A.M. STERN ARCHITECTS

K. C. IRVING ENVIRONMENTAL SCIENCE CENTER
AND HARRIET IRVING BOTANICAL GARDENS

Acadia University
Wolfville, Nova Scotia, Canada 2002

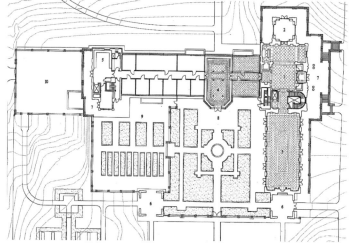

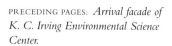

The K. C. Irving Environmental Science Center adds 65,000 square feet of research facilities, instructional space, and ceremonial reception rooms to Acadia University. With its red brick facade, granite water table, limestone trim, and slate roof, the restrained Georgian style of the new complex matches the established character of the campus. The lighted cupola orients the internal circulation of the building and also terminates the visual and pedestrian axes of the historic University Hall and the Students' Center. The lower level contains an auditorium and classroom spaces. The main level contains a main reception/lounge area that opens to the walled garden and the Acadia Room, a 2,400-square-foot reception space with views across the botanical gardens and the Bay of Fundy. Included among the building's research facilities is a greenhouse and a 4,500-square-foot archival herbarium that contains a collection of over 400,000 preserved botanical specimens dating back to the eighteenth century. The Harriet Irving Botanical Gardens include a walled garden, graduation lawn, and research garden dedicated to the study of native flora of the Acadia region.

ROBERT A.M. STERN ARCHITECTS

NASHVILLE PUBLIC LIBRARY

Nashville, Tennessee, 2001

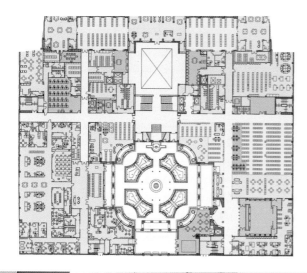

Located on a bluff above the Cumberland River, the city of Nashville rises dramatically to the towering location of the Tennessee state capitol, designed by William Strickland. Situated on axis with the nineteenth-century capitol, the Nashville Public Library's design reinforces the coherence of the government district through similar materials and classical detailing. Located on the ridge above the city, the library economically accommodates the steeply sloping site by virtue of the architects' placing portions of the upper two floors on top of an existing parking structure. Clear orientation within the complex public library system's main building is maintained through axial organization and a series of courts. Entering from the axis of the capitol, the visitor is drawn through the two-story entry lobby toward the skylit main stair hall. The interior reading rooms orient to the second floor open-air landscaped courtyard. Like the great libraries of the past—Ste. Genevieve in Paris, and the Boston and New York public libraries— the Nashville library design incorporates symbolic art throughout the building and includes work by muralist Richard Haas and sculptor Kent Bloomer.

LEFT: *Grand Reading Room designed in the tradition of America's monumental public reading rooms found in Boston and New York.*

RIGHT (TOP): *The Nashville Room provides space for temporary exhibitions like these costumed mannequins.*

RIGHT (BOTTOM): *Civil Rights Reading Room.*

213

DAVID M. SCHWARZ
ARCHITECTURAL SERVICES, INC.

David Schwarz's firm typifies the eclectic trend in current architectural practice in America. The diverse project types, scales, and locations encountered by the firm encourage equally diverse design responses. Schwarz attributes his willingness to choose among modern, postmodern, traditional, or classical styles to the time period of his education. Schwarz first received a liberal arts degree from St. John's College in Annapolis, Maryland, and then a master's of architecture from Yale University (1974). At Yale, history professor Vincent Scully and design professor Charles Moore greatly affected his knowledge and understanding of architecture. About the influence of Scully and Moore, Schwarz says, "Both men were very well-versed in classicism and both men had deep roots in architectural history. I think it was through them that I grew to understand the importance of understanding our history to finding our place in the present and helping to map a better future. For my firm, style is just one of the many tools that an architect has to make manifest a client's dreams and a building's purpose." Equally influential on his future practice were his classmates Andreas Duany and Elizabeth Plater-Zyberk, the founders of the New Urbanism movement.

The firm's offices in Washington, D.C. (opened in 1976), and Ft. Worth, Texas (opened in 1985), design primarily large-scale institutional, commercial, sports, and educational facilities. When he opened his office, Schwarz looked closely at the organization of firms he admired, especially those of Caesar Pelli and Robert A. M. Stern. From those two firms, Schwarz learned that it was possible to resist specialization in a single type or scale of project. At St. John's College he absorbed the philosophy that an educated man could learn anything. Through looking at other firms, Schwarz decided to modify this philosophy to "A good designer can design anything." He also transferred this philosophy to his involvement in teaching. He feels that interacting with students creates a crucial dialogue around important design issues.

Characteristic of their use of historic inspiration, the stadium in Arlington, built for the Texas Rangers baseball team (1994), replaces the enormous scale of the modernist corporate stadium with an old-style baseball park whose design brings the fan closer to the ballgame and whose appearance references the brick detailing of an earlier era of entertainment grandstands. The Nancy Lee and Perry R. Bass Performance Hall in Fort Worth includes angelic heralds whose legible ornament gives specific identity to this public building. Such a move away from minimalist and functionally unreadable buildings fulfills a desire for architecture that allows many levels of interpretation in addition to form, mass, and finish. Like many of the more traditional classical firms, David Schwarz also works in historic preservation, renovation, and adaptive reuse.

DAVID M. SCHWARZ/ ARCHITECTURAL SERVICES, INC.

FORT WORTH CENTRAL LIBRARY

Fort Worth, Texas, 1999

PRECEDING PAGES: *New south facade, Fort Worth Central Library.*

LEFT (TOP): *Detail of new south facade.*

LEFT (BOTTOM): *Ground floor plan of the new library.*

OPPOSITE: *Main entrance on the north facade.*

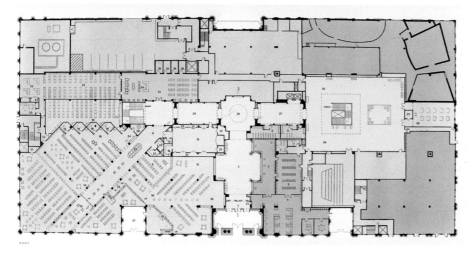

As an innovative solution to correct leakage problems in a 1970s two-square-block, underground library, the client requested a new two-story shell to cover the entire site. The new Fort Worth Central Library solved the water penetration problems and provided much needed expansion space. The new exterior pays homage to Fort Worth's original Carnegie Library, which had been demolished. The construction budget was extremely limited, but the design achieves a sense of permanence and civic importance appropriate for a central library. Because the original Carnegie libraries were usually made of marble, the appearance of stone was effectively simulated here with an exterior insulated finish system and glass fiber reinforced concrete.

In order to fit the 460 feet of building facade with the existing scale of the surrounding city fabric, the design created an appearance of three connected buildings. The monumental entry, with a pediment supported on coupled columns, separates two-story wings that have the scale of a small commercial row. The second phase of the project included 50,000 square feet of interior space incorporating a 6,000-square-foot media library and a 20,000-square-foot youth library.

The Hazel Harvey Peace Youth Center

TOP (LEFT): *The grand entrance lobby continues the scale of the giant orders of the main entrance. Floor and wainscot are honed and flame-finished French-Corton limestone.*

BOTTOM (LEFT): *Circulation sequence connecting east, west, and central lobbies.*

BOTTOM (RIGHT): *The rainbow archway marks entrance to the youth center and diagonal circulation path.*

OPPOSITE: *The second story of the grand entrance lobby with spandrels symbolically detailed with open books and quill pens.*

DAVID M. SCHWARZ/ ARCHITECTURAL
SERVICES, INC.

NANCY LEE AND PERRY R.
BASS PERFORMANCE HALL
Fort Worth, Texas, 1998

PRECEDING PAGES: *Main elevation of the performance hall.*

LEFT: *Corner entrance.*

BOTTOM (RIGHT): *Ground floor plan.*

OPPOSITE: *Forty-eight-foot-tall angel sculpted from Cordova crème Texas limestone by Márton Váró.*

The Nancy Lee and Perry R. Bass Performance Hall serves as the new home of the Fort Worth Symphony, the Fort Worth Opera, and the Fort Worth Ballet, and hosts the quadrennial Van Cliburn International Piano Competition and incoming performances and traveling Broadway productions. The hall can be configured for different performances, and seats between 2,000 and 2,100 patrons.

The limited downtown city block site required imaginative planning. Located in the Sundance neighborhood, Fort Worth's emerging nightlife district, the mass of the auditorium is stepped down in scale to address the pedestrian areas. The lobby has two entries that also scale down to the shops, restaurants, and clubs in the Sundance community. The building's function as the centerpiece of the district is signified by the two-story winged sculptures that dramatically announce this is a center of the performing arts.

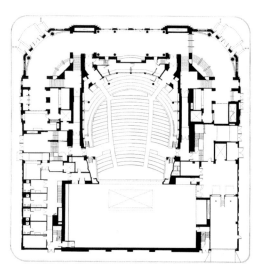

BELOW: *Orchestra level grand lobby.*

OPPOSITE: *West entry lobby with vaulted ceiling symbolically painted with Texas flora and fauna by Scott and Stuart Gentling.*

BELOW: *The acoustical shell set up for symphony. The towers and ceiling can be stored for opera, musicals, and rock concerts.*

OPPOSITE: *The horseshoe-shaped tiers of seating in the Founders Concert Theater are topped by Scott and Stuart Gentling's dome murals depicting a wreath of white angel feathers embracing a central oculus of brilliant Texas sky.*

DAVID M. SCHWARZ/ ARCHITECTURAL SERVICES, INC.

SEVERANCE HALL

Cleveland, Ohio, 1999

PRECEDING PAGES: *The new five-story addition located to the back of the original Severance Hall (1931) creates a new plaza focus for Case Western Reserve University.*

BELOW (LEFT): *Restaurant patio in new addition.*

BELOW (RIGHT): *Ground floor plan.*

OPPOSITE: *New plaza facade with "Severance" orders composed of Ionic volutes symbolically adapted with inverted treble clefs, organ keyboards, lotus buds, and Riesling grape clusters.*

The work at Severance Hall, Cleveland, Ohio, included a 42,000-square-foot restoration and a 39,000-square-foot expansion of the landmark home of the Cleveland Orchestra. The original 1931 neoclassical building designed by Walker and Weeks had been damaged by incompatible additions in 1958. The eclectic Art Deco, classical, and Egyptian Revival interiors were restored, and a compatible vocabulary reflecting these styles was created for the new additions. This project received numerous professional awards including the 2001 National Preservation Award from the National Trust for Historic Preservation, a 2001 Honor Award from the U.S. Institute for Theatre Technology, and the 2000 American Institute of Architects Washington Chapter Award of Merit in Historical Resources.

BELOW: *View of the Ong Gallery. Varying room shapes and materials modulate a new entry connecting underground parking with the new Smith lobby. The three types of Spanish marble found in the original building are incorporated in the new parallel halls.*

OPPOSITE: *Restored Bogomoly-Kozerefski Grand Foyer*

BELOW: *View of new Severance—The Restaurant.*

OPPOSITE: *View of the restored Rankin Board Room with portrait of Alfred M. Rankin, longtime board president.*

FOLLOWING PAGES: *View of the restored house and proscenium arch, and new concert platform designed to harmoniously fit with the earlier detailing. The center focus of the rear stage wall are non-speaking pipes that reference the 6,025 unseen pipes of the restored Norton Memorial organ designed in 1930 by Ernest M. Skinner of Boston.*

NOTES

Robert Adam Architects
page 26
1. Robert Adam, "Invention, Modernity and the Classical Tradition," in Richard Economakis, ed., *Building Classical: A Vision of Europe and America* (London: Academy Editions, 1993), p. 197.
2. Robert Adam, *Classical Architecture: A Complete Handbook* (New York: Harry N. Abrams, 1990), p. 1.

Julian Bicknell & Associates
page 48
1. Julian Bicknell, "Introduction," *Julian Bicknell: designs and buildings 1980–2000*, January 2000.

Quinlan & Francis Terry
page 80
1. Taken from a speech given at the Oxford Union Debate, November 1987. Published in *The Salisbury Review*, June 1988, and *Quinlan Terry: Selected Works* (London: Academy Editions, 1993), p. 132.

Fairfax and Sammons
page 94
1. Eve M. Kahn, "Lyrical Compositions," *Period Homes*, Spring 2003, Vol 4., No. 1, p. 1.

John Simpson & Partners
page 108
1. Richard John and David Watkin, *John Simpson: The Queen's Gallery, Buckingham Palace and Other Works* (London: Andreas Papadakis, 2002), p. 11.
2. ibid. p.14.

Allan Greenberg Architect
page 138
1. Allan Greenberg, "The Architecture of Democracy," *New Classicism* (New York, Rizzoli International, 1990), and Allan Greenberg, *George Washington Architect* (London: Andreas Papadakis Publisher, 1999), pp. 69-72.
2. Lubow, Arthur, "The Ionic Man," *Departures Magazine*, May/June, 1999, pp. 156-157.
3. Allan Greenberg, "The Architecture of Democracy," *New Classicism* (New York, Rizzoli International, 1990), p. 72.

Robert A. M. Stern Architects
page 202
1. *Robert A. M. Stern Buildings* (New York: Monacelli Press, 1996), p. 17.

PHOTOGRAPHY CREDITS

© Peter Aaron/Esto 202, 203, 204, 205, 206, 207, 208, 209, 210, 211, 212, 213

ArFam/Georgian Club 56, 57, 58, 59

John Blatteau Associates 72

Hedrich Blessing 214, 215, 216, 217, 218, 219, 220, 221, 222, 223, 224, 225, 226, 227, 228, 229, 230, 231, 232, 233, 234, 235, 236, 237, 238, 239

Tim Buchman 2, 3, 8, 138, 139, 144, 145, 146, 147, 148, 149, 150, 151

Nick Carter Back jacket, 80, 81, 82, 83, 84, 85, 86, 87, 88, 89

Richard Cheek 13 14 15

Tom Crane/ Jeffrey Totaro 71, 73, 74, 75

Phillip Ennis 122, 123

Mark Feinnes 48

Brian Gassel 34, 35, 42, 43, 44, 45, 46, 47

Mick Hales 124, 125, 126, 127, 128, 129, 130, 131, 132, 133, 134, 135, 136, 137

© 2003 Hester + Hardaway 188, 189, 192, 193, 194, 195, 196, 197, 198, 199, 200, 201

Robert Lautman 140, 141, 142, 143

Joe Low 32, 33

Alberto Muciaccia 26, 27, 28, 29, 30, 31

© Porphyrios Associates 152, 153, 154, 155, 156, 157, 158, 159, 160, 161, 162, 163, 164, 165, 166, 167, 168, 169

The Royal Collection © 2003, Her Majesty Queen Elizabeth II 5, 108, 110, 111, 112, 113, 114, 115, 116, 117

2003 SARGENT Architectural Photography 36, 37, 38, 39, 40, 41

© 1998 Durston Saylor 95, 102, 103, 104, 105, 106, 107

© 2003 Durston Saylor 96, 97, 98, 99, 100, 101

Fritz von Schulenberg/Julian Bicknell 64, 65, 66, 67, 68, 69

John Simpson and Partners 109, 118, 119, 120, 121

Swan Group 49, 50, 51, 52, 53, 54, 55

John Umberger – Real Images Cover, 170, 171, 172, 173, 174, 175, 176, 177, 178, 179, 180, 181, 182, 183, 184, 185, 186, 187

Matt Wargo 70, 76, 77, 78, 79

Neil Waving 90, 91, 92, 93

Wiltshiers/Julian Bicknell 60, 61, 62, 63